SPEAKING OF
THE HOLY

SPEAKING OF THE HOLY

THE ART OF COMMUNICATION IN PREACHING

Richard F. Ward

CHALICE PRESS

ST. LOUIS, MISSOURI

© Copyright 2001 by Richard F. Ward

All rights reserved. No part of this book may be reproduced without written permission from Chalice Press, P.O. Box 179, St. Louis, MO 63166-0179.

Biblical quotations, unless otherwise noted, are from the *New Revised Standard Version Bible*, copyright 1989, Division of Christian Education of the National Council of the Churches of Christ in the United States of America. Used by permission. All rights reserved.

Excerpts from "The Cosmos Is His Sanctuary (Psalm 50)" by Ernesto Cardinal, translated by Donald D. Walsh, is from APOCALYPSE AND OTHER POEMS, copyright © 1977 by Ernesto Cardinal and Donald D. Walsh. Reprinted by permission of New Directions Publishing Corp.

Excerpts from "Church Going" by Philip Larkin are reprinted from *The Less Deceived* by permission of The Marvell Press, England and Australia.

Cover design: Wendy Barnes
Interior design: Elizabeth Wright
Art direction: Elizabeth Wright

This book is printed on acid-free, recycled paper.

Visit Chalice Press on the World Wide Web at
www.chalicepress.com

10 9 8 7 6 5 4 3 2 1   01 02 03

Library of Congress Cataloging–in–Publication Data

Ward, Richard F.
    Speaking of the holy : the art of communication in preaching / Richard F. Ward.
        p.   cm.
    Includes bibliographical references.
    ISBN 0-8272-3448-1 (alk. paper)
    1. Preaching.   I. Title.
BV4211.3 .W37   2001
251–dc21   2001005043

Printed in the United States of America

CONTENTS

Introduction   1

1 What Communication Means for Preaching   17
  and Proclamation
  WORKSHOP 1: Public Reading as a Communicative Act 30

2 Speaking and Hearing a "Lively Word"   33
  WORKSHOP 2: Public Reading as an Interpretive Act   44

3 The First R: Reading Your Text   47
  WORKSHOP 3: Public Reading as a Communicative Art 66

4 The Second R: The Recitation of Scripture   71

5 The Third R: Retelling Stories from Scripture   89

Conclusion   117

Epilogue   123

Notes   129

INTRODUCTION

ENTERING THE SILENCE

This book started as a meditation on a breeze blowing through an empty church. I was driving on a stretch of highway in rural Indiana when I saw the church, sitting on the edge of a cornfield. It was harvest time; the stalks were bulging with their fruit and had invaded the churchyard. I stopped the car and turned around. I found what was left of the driveway and parked.

It was clear that the place had not been used for a long time. Perhaps the families that once worshiped here had moved, and no one was left to take their places in the pews. There was a well-tended graveyard nearby. The door was not locked, so I let myself in. A few of the old pews were turned over and laid on their backs. I spoke loud enough from the back door to try out the acoustics but not to attract unwanted attention.

There was a lot of paper lying around, and pieces of old hymnbooks. On the door of a classroom was a piece of green felt cut in the shape of a banner that said, "Banner Class Attendance." I remembered a poem by Philip Larkin while I stood there; the poem is entitled "Church Going." The speaker in that poem also enters an empty church and tells us

> Once I am sure there's nothing going on
> I step inside, letting the door thud shut.
> Another church: matting, seats, and stone,
> And little books; sprawlings of flowers, cut
> For Sunday, brownish now; some brass and stuff
> Up at the holy end; the small neat organ;
> And a tense, musty, unignorable silence,
> Brewed God knows how long.[1]

I moved to one of the windows and opened it. The fresh winds that blew from across the cornfield disrupted the "unignorable silence" of the space I had entered. I thought of how winds are indeed blowing through the congregations where we worship. New technologies are shaping our very ways of listening to and speaking of God together, and they are causing us to think again about the use of old books and pieces of paper. Some want to tighten their grip on the books before the pages blow out of their hands. Others are happy to be liberated, not only from print, but also from the liturgical traditions and ways of speaking and acting in worship that print has represented. We are living in a whirlwind of change, not sure of what to do with printed pages, but more than that, not sure of what kinds of speech and actions are appropriate for worship in these emerging contexts. Is worship to be more boisterous? Or is worship a place to find some sanctuary from all the noise that the new electronic media make? What do we expect from worship these days? What competencies do worship leaders need to have?

Those who plan, lead, and/or preach in corporate worship often use the word *style*. Although there are some suspicions about that word, *style* is a good word to use when we talk about leadership in worship. It describes a manner of being present before God and before the people gathered to worship God. It points to a complex coalescence of personality, competence, and confidence in leading a congregation through a worship experience. It is difficult for busy pastors and lay readers to stop for a moment and ask the question, What is a *good* and effective style of worship leadership? Michael DeVito gives some suggestions on what to value in one's "presidential style."[2] He tells us that "presidential style" is the manner in which we conduct the congregation through the performance of its liturgy. The one who presides in communal worship does so with love, reverence, and humility, "in the person of Christ over the celebration of Christ's ministry and the people's."[3] To cultivate one's style is to maintain a life of prayerful presence before God, to understand the purposes and intentions of worship, and to become aware of one's posture, gestures, and eye contact with those he or she is leading in worship.

Developing an effective presidential style means paying conscious attention to the variety of ways we speak in worship, including invocations, calls to prayer, prayers of confession and intercession, offertory prayers, and benedictions. This book focuses on the communicative values of scripture and sermon in worship. How the pastor prepares the scripture readers for their part in worship, or prepares him- or herself for speaking the text and the sermon, either deepens or diminishes the participation of all who worship.

BY THE LETTER OR BY THE SPIRIT?

Let's take a quick look at the kinds of paper that the winds of this technological age are blowing around in the churches where we worship. What do we do with the printed pages of the scriptures and the sermon manuscript? How do we read the scriptures in ways that are full of intention and purpose? How will we preach in this whirlwind of change? How will our preaching arise from the printed words we read aloud together in worship or in the silence of our studies? The winds that were blowing through that empty church that day were like spirits that went where they would! How do we discern which of these "spirits" are accountable to the "Spirit" we Christians call "Holy"? This book will suggest that we keep at least one foot grounded in traditions of communication and expression that have guided us through media changes before. The traditions of interpretive reading, speaking, and worshiping together help us discern what is a fickle breeze and what is the steady reliable wind of the Spirit.

To meet the challenges presented in this age, we need not simply discard the paper that guides our worship or further devalue liturgical traditions that do not readily appeal to "seekers." Nor should we continue our conventional practices of reading and speaking as if the winds had not blown through our particular church. We do need to reassess how we use the medium of print in the acts of speaking and reading aloud. Reassessing the relationship between speech and print means remembering the impact that oral communication of the printed word has made on our lives.

THE MAKING OF A PREACHER

I walked up to the place where the pulpit had been (the marks were still impressed in the faded carpet). Larkin's speaker also makes this move:

Mounting the lectern, I peruse a few
Hectoring large-scale verses, and pronounce
'Here endeth' much more loudly than I'd meant.
The echoes snigger briefly.[4]

I pronounced a few words to the long-departed congregation, and as I did, I remembered that preaching had once been a form of play for me. On Saturday afternoons I would walk from the parsonage, down the alley and around the block, and go into the church with my father. While he labored in the quiet of his study to put the final touches on his sermon, I wandered into the empty sanctuary to play at being a preacher. I would pace around the platform, trying on different voices and behaviors, until I came up with some ragged thread of an idea. Some words would come, then some crude elements of form. I would feel some strange stirrings of energy. Very soon I would be doing a free fall through a web of language, stories, images, and ideas.

I shudder now to think what all that raw, undisciplined exploration sounded like. What if someone had been present to put all that on tape? How embarrassed I would feel if I were forced to watch or listen to a playback of those early explorations today. Yet sometimes I wonder if indeed some bemused, invisible "cloud of witnesses" was present in spirit on those occasions to urge me on. It reminds me today of how human we are and must be when we preach. We are playful, feeling a bit foolish, yet serious enough to give our voices, bodies, imaginations, and childlike hearts to what it is that moves us to speak. We respond to a Holy Spirit that we understand only in part. Yet we preachers try to respond with the totality of our lives.

I finally got the courage to tell my father what I was doing in the sanctuary while he was down in his study. I was afraid he would chuckle at my childish behaviors. Instead, he smiled and said that when he was a boy, he used to go far out into the fields of the farm behind his house and there preach to the cows as they grazed in the pasture. What an image of preaching THAT could be! It was there, in those early, playful explorations in that empty sanctuary that I became interested in being a preacher.

That old abandoned church was a good place to remember that all of us who preach arrive at the pulpit by very different paths. It may seem that some of us get there by some unlikely routes. David Bartlett reminds us that all those who find themselves teaching, writing about, and/or practicing the art of preaching these days need to make their biases explicit and speak about what influenced them.[5] In this book I show how one set of biases and explorations grew up and became convictions about preaching as communication and art.

PREACHING AS PERFORMANCE, COMMUNICATION, AND ART

I have come to believe that preaching is performance, a complex of creative processes that punctuate the preparation, enactment, and embodiment of sermons. Preaching calls on inspiration, but also depends on a variety of competencies and skills. There are a number of windows open in the homiletical household that are letting fresh breezes in. We enjoy a broad conceptual openness in our collective study of preaching; there are no reigning "orthodoxies." Homiletics allows itself to be approached from many different angles–biblical, theological, and historical–but only if one assumes a posture of humility when entering the conversation. I was trained in the discipline of performance studies, a discipline that also exhibits expansionist tendencies.

Performance studies arises out of many disciplines of inquiry, but I am most influenced by one of its traditional antecedents, the oral study and performance of literature. Performance studies is based on the concept that human beings are *homo performans*, that is, those creatures who define themselves to themselves and to one another through an infinite array of verbal and gestural enactments within and throughout individual and collective ritual and aesthetic acts. Performance studies resists tendencies in the humanities and in theology to narrowly and pejoratively construe performance as mere sham or fakery. Instead, performance studies builds its research and practice on a view that human activity can be studied in reference to traditions of enactment, expression, and embodiment. "Through performance," write Carol Simpson Stern and Bruce Henderson, "one can both live through primary social processes and reflect back on them, investing them with meaning."[6]

These *constructive* views of performance have guided my own thinking about preaching and reading scripture aloud as communicative behavior. The transaction that takes place between the preacher, the text, the listener, and God can be imagined as a shifting field of relationships that receive emphasis at different points in the performative process.

For example, when a reader stands to present a text in a worship service, that reader is communicating a complex of messages to an audience. The emphasis is on the text itself, the emotions, thoughts, ideas, and attitudes that are present in and through the text. There is also an emphasis on the one who is presenting the text. The reader, who is highly visible to the listener (as he or she is standing in a place designated for the purpose of public reading), through his or her voice, gesture, and attitude reveals the level of understanding, reverence, and effect that the text has had on him or her. Unfortunately for our listeners, these values and dynamics rarely operate in ways that make the meaning of a text clear or evoke the kind of response that a public reading of scripture deserves. The reading should shift our attention to the question, What might God have to say to this gathered group through the reading of these words? Instead, the occasion calls attention to the reader's lack of preparation, the vast distance between the world of the text and the listener's own, and the amount of time it takes to simply get to something more interesting. This creates very little anticipation in the mind and heart of the listener to hear what the preacher might have to say on this particular text.

On the matter of "speaking" the sermon, I am growing increasingly restless with the term *delivery*. Preaching is not simply the opportunity to *deliver* the goods from the pulpit by means of the voice and body. *Performance* is a richer, more integrative way of describing how primary elements of language and form coalesce with the actions of speech, gesture, and embodiment in the preaching event. In the mind and experience of both the preacher and the listener, the performance of the scripture and the performance of the sermon are intertwined with the structure of worship. Within and throughout these performances, the listener may hear deep resonances and dissonances, echoes and silences. Readings that do not take the communicative values of a text seriously place added burdens on the performance of the sermon and the ability of the listener to "make sense" out of what was read and heard in the gathering. Conversely, a sermon that fails to take the oral/aural quality of the scripture seriously (whether in the sanctuary or the study) flattens the effect that scripture and sermon can have in the listener's imagination.

Preaching is also an *artful* way to speak of the Holy. When we are describing preaching as *art*, we point to the way that a preacher leads her or his listeners into an experience of the Word through the use of language and imagery, designing the sermon into a coherent and organic whole. *Communication* usually describes the ways that the voice and body are used in preaching. The boundaries between *communication* and *art* are increasingly being blurred in the study and practice of preaching, but they point to two qualities of the preaching event itself: *Preaching arises out of the God-given impulse to "do things with words" in bearing witness to God's own self-disclosure in Jesus Christ. Yet that very impulse to "create" becomes directed toward others in the public spaces we have designated for corporate worship.*

Art and *communication* are two terms that describe what we aim for, but I think we would all agree with Elizabeth Achtemeier:

> It is true to say that preaching at the present time is rarely artistic, because many preachers, while good journeymen, have not become true masters of the English language. Involved in the artistic use of English are timing and rhythm and sound, and many preachers have no knowledge of the importance of these characteristics of speech for riveting attention and carrying along a congregation and touching their hearts as well as their minds.[7]

Performance studies' legacy of creating, evaluating, and *doing* performances is a resource for homiletics, because it addresses this problem of integrating language, sound, and movement in an oral, interpretive act of human communication. Like preaching, its concern is with the interrelationships between different forms of human utterance—framed variously as literary texts, human speech, or rituals—and embodiment. One recurring subject you will find in this book is the interrelationships between preaching and the other *oral* arts, such as public scripture reading, recitation, and biblical storytelling, within the ministry of proclamation.

As in theology, some practitioners of performance studies take an interest in the ways that human beings address one another and God. One operative metaphor in the discipline is *logos,* or the image of Word becoming enfleshed and acknowledged as the presence of the "Word's Body."[8] Enfleshment and embodiment are understood as dramatic disclosures of the Other. A performance-centered view of human speaking displays preaching as an "anguished striving for authenticity"[9] and emphasizes the role of speech and gesture in the creation of shared meanings, mutuality, and engagement.

My early explorations of preaching were playful and improvisational, representing an intuitive search for forms and structures of speech and thought. Later, I became intrigued by a different kind of "play," that of making connections between preaching and other forms of expressive speech, specifically oral interpretation and storytelling. I found that the practice of preparing texts for public performance trained my eyes and ears differently than did silent, critical reading of texts. The commitment to orally present texts changed the kinds of questions I would ask when I was trying to grasp what a text meant. I began to wonder how I might more fully approach and enter the perceptual world described by a text by asking certain questions:

- What emotional, psychological, and intellectual effect does this constellation of language, structure, and gesture have on me?
- What does the author (that is present in this text) seem to want to accomplish in the spiritual, sociopolitical, and everyday life of his or her own community?
- How am I implicated as a reader of these texts at such a great distance in space and time?
- What kinds of claims do these texts have on me and those I address as I use these words?

These questions arise from a lifelong fascination with the emotional effect and intellectual impact that spoken scripture has on various audiences.

BECOMING A READER OF SCRIPTURE:
A PERSONAL HISTORY

The scene is a Baptist church in Colonial Heights, Virginia, a bedroom community for Richmond. It is early June, and the large sanctuary is filled with warm and brilliant sunlight. It is the opening ceremony for vacation Bible school, and the students are standing at attention in the rows of pews. Two preadolescent boys are standing on either side of the large white pulpit, each one awkwardly but respectfully holding a flag. One holds the flag of the United States. The other boy holds the "Christian" flag, consisting of a field of blue with a red cross in a white square in the upper left-hand corner. Standing down on the red carpet in front of the pulpit is a nervous young girl who is holding open a heavy black, shiny Bible.

The students, recently emancipated from the "regular" school year, are now herded into the sanctuary on this bright June morning, and they restlessly shift their weight as the respective pledges of allegiance to the flags are said. Then their attention shifts to the open Bible. The instruction comes gently, but with a firm authority: "Attention!" (the effort to stand up straight for the third time); "Salute!" (the right hand comes up to the heart); "Pledge!"

I pledge allegiance to the Bible,
God's Holy Word,
And will make it a lamp unto my feet,
A light unto my path,
And will hide its words in my heart
That I might not sin against God.

The pianist strikes the first chords of a hymn that the congregation virtually knows by heart:

Holy Bible book divine
Precious treasure thou art mine
Mine to tell me whence I came
Mine to teach me who I am.

The fact that I can still remember the words and the tune to that song, performed in the church of my youth, impresses me.

One of the most valued expressions of faithfulness in that community was the careful cultivation of knowledge of the Bible through diligent personal reading and study. These and other claims made about the importance of reading the Bible drew me into a lifelong relationship with it. I remember the size of that Bible lying open in that nervous child's arms and understood it as a gateway to the most deeply held values and convictions of that community of faith. Reading the scriptures for oneself was a highly regarded expression of piety and an enactment of one's freedom in Christ to interpret sacred matters for oneself.

There was another practice related to reading the scriptures in silence. *Reciting* the scripture from memory was a highly valued discipline. Those children and adults in the community who worked at memorizing specific scriptures in order to speak them aloud were recognized and rewarded. Memorizing, reciting, and orally interpreting what the scripture meant demonstrated one's "knowledge of the Bible."

Such practices were held up for scrutiny by some and for ridicule by others. Memorizing scripture was often a substitute for critical engagement with those texts and was not the same as deep knowledge of them. Oftentimes particular interpretations were internalized with the texts, making it difficult to look at them from other interpretive angles. Memorizing scripture reinforced the notion that the biblical text could somehow "speak for itself" and did not require interpretation. The style of speaking simply encouraged rote recitation, that is, an oral/aural re-creation of what appeared on the page. What you heard was stilted, forced, and hurried, and featured the speaker's command of the words of the text, but not much of its thought and meaning. Methods for memorizing were often fun, but sometimes were tinged with fear and intimidation. Many people's taste for biblical study was soured by these experiences of forced memorization. By the time I got to seminary, there were no serious attempts there at an "oral" study of scripture.

As problematic as these methods were, I was left with a memory of the Bible that is full of sound and movement and is interwoven with memories of my community. I remember the sounds of a visiting preacher's voice, but also the sound of scripture in the mouths of my teachers and family members. The Bible was a vital, living source for speaking of God to one another when our own language failed us. The Bible prompted interest and enthusiasm, even forms of play.

It was also a book; in fact, it was deemed to be the greatest of all books of religious experience. The Bible was the place one went to know God. God's character, God's promises, and the history of God's actions were explained there. Learning to read meant gaining access to the greatest mysteries of faith, and indeed of life itself. Baptists believed that biblical writers spoke to us of God and gave us directions on how to find God.[10] We read not simply for information but for transformation, since "regeneration" was evidence of the ongoing work of Jesus Christ, whose deeds were anticipated and then revealed in the writings.

The person and work of Jesus were central to God's message to humankind. The New Testament was taken to be the only authoritative source of the works of salvation Jesus had done in his earthly ministry and the implications that work had for Christian conduct. One read of these things to find correspondences between his or her own life and the saving work of grace disclosed by the scriptures themselves.

What gave vitality to the reading was assent not simply to that which was written but to what that knowledge contributed to one's own existence and identity as a Christian. What gave the Bible its authority was the "truth" that was revealed in the soul of the individual and that which was given in scripture. So we experienced our lives as being tightly braided with the "life" presented in scripture. No wonder we children stood with our hands over our hearts to pledge "allegiance" to the "precious treasure" that had been given to us by God! No wonder resurgent fundamentalists place such an emphasis on "getting into the Word" for the individual believer!

It took me some years to discover that the reader's experience of texts and biblical imagination was constrained by some rather tightly held theological propositions that blinded one to other regions of human religious experience, not the least of which was a doctrine about the Bible itself. Claims are often made that the Bible speaks with authority in matters beyond the terrain of the life of faith, including science and history; it even mapped the future! Biblical history moves toward a vanishing point wherein

Jesus Christ appears at the end of Time itself to "judge the quick and the dead." Tragically, those who did not assent to "what the Bible said" would be consigned to perdition for all eternity. A popular bumper sticker expresses it best: "The Bible says it, I believe it, that settles it!"

One had best learn to read! So we read as if our lives (and our souls) depended on it. We read as if our lives would be *found* there in the biblical texts. Some other communities of faith found grace in the sacraments of baptism or bread and wine; in our community, reading was our sacrament (though we wouldn't have used that term!). It was spiritual "food." "As newborn babes, desire the sincere milk of the word, that ye may grow thereby" (1 Pet. 2:2 KJV). For us in that suburban church on that street corner in white America, the Bible became the prism, the "precious treasure" through which we looked at ourselves, the world in which we found ourselves, and the future that lay on the horizon. Unfortunately, the Bible was also used to shore up opinions that blinded us to the kinds of oppression we were participating in as white Americans, locked in structures of exclusion.

The practices and techniques of historical criticism helped sustain the Bible's capacity not only to speak to my experience, but also to challenge me with new perspectives. I remember that as a college senior I gathered with some of my friends for a Bible study that freely employed historical critical methods. We studied the times, circumstances, and situations that elicited and provoked the writing and production of the texts we selected for study. I remember leaving those gatherings excited and refreshed and anxious to enter seminary. Reading texts in this way released them from flat literalism, restored the power of these texts to call me and my friends to deeper faith and obedience and, in fact, nourished a call in many of us to Christian ministry.

Reading the biblical text through eyes trained by historical critical methods opened up the texts in fresh ways, but also placed us squarely on a battlefront. The battle over the Bible and the nature of its authority became something that we argued with our more conservative friends, and we suffered some casualties in the ranks of readers. They were worried we would "lose our faith" if we continued to study the Bible in these ways. For some, the casualty was one's own denominational identity. For others, the relationship to the Bible itself became a casualty in these ongoing battles. The passionate reader could not escape the dilemma: the more one became interested in the Word of God through reading and study, the more the Bible became a problem. The greater the focus on the problems presented, the greater the risk of losing one's grip on the Bible-as-Word-of-God. So wounded were some students of the Bible that they lost confidence in it altogether and broke off their relationship with it.

I recall that story here because I find myself among others who wonder how we can "recover the Bible's power to take captive the imagination of readers and interpreters."[11] I am among others who wonder how the Bible became "strangely silent." "Strange silence" has proven to be a durable description for the status of Bible study in many churches. James Smart first coined the phrase in 1970 with a book that wondered why "mainline" churches seemed to have lost interest in studying scripture.[12] Donald Juel recently recalled Smart's phrase in making the point more explicit: "The oral/aural power of the Bible has been strangely neglected within the worship life of the church as well as in recent biblical scholarship"[13] One hope I express in this book is that the "silence" that inhibits the Bible's capacity to speak in, through, and for the church might be overcome. A vibrant tradition of scholarship and practice is available to point us to some ways of overcoming this strange and persistent silence. In the community of scholars, that tradition is identified by various names: "oral interpretation," "interpretation of literature," "biblical storytelling," "performance of texts," or simply, "performance studies." Mining that tradition will nourish the community's study and practice of scripture and the preacher's capacity not only to return biblical texts to living human speech but also to refresh the preacher's homiletical imagination.

This is the conviction that gives rise to this book. My aim is to encourage preachers to cultivate a relationship to scripture that respects its "orality" and thereby pursue a fresh and more imaginative engagement with it and benefit from its evocative power. Discovering the value of an oral hermeneutic of scripture–emanating from a conviction that performing scripture opens up new horizons for interpreting it–refreshed and renewed my own relationship to scripture and made me want to preach from it again after a long and strange silence. The practice of oral reading did more than simply prepare me and others to make our own public performance of scripture more "interesting." Reading the Bible aloud, whether in the privacy of my own study or in the congregation, changed the way that I engaged scripture and the way it engaged me.

The Spirit is blowing through our congregations and is equipping people for new kinds of praise and proclamation. The final psalm in the collection, number 150, takes as its subject the technologies of praise. Trumpets, lutes, harps, tambourines, strings, and pipes are mentioned along with dance and breath as means of performing praise. Ernesto Cardenal, a Latin American theologian and poet, amplifies the psalmist's theme:

Praise Him with blues and jazz
and with symphonic orchestras
with Negro spirituals
and with Beethoven's Fifth
with guitars and marimbas
Praise Him with record players
and with magnetic tapes
Let everything that breathes praise the Lord
every living cell
Hallelujah[14]

This is not the time to close the window to the Spirit and grab what is left over from a former technological age. It is not the time to pull the plug on our electronic instruments, nor is it time to throw away all our books, our printed matter, or the idea of preaching off a page. It is time to remember what the purpose and goal of worship is and how we use what is available to us to perform our speech and praise in this time and place.

Just before I left that old church, I picked up a children's Bible that the wind had blown over into a corner. Some pages were missing, but I kept it anyway. I kept it as a reminder of how important the Bible was to me in my childhood but also as a reminder that from time to time we need to "become as little children again" in order to renew our relationships to our scriptures. I remember how indebted I was to the orality of scripture, how it lived for me in song, ritual, celebration, and ceremony—not quiet and still—printed but not confined to a page in a book. I am concerned that our experience of scripture is getting smaller and smaller, its place in our memory rapidly eclipsed by new and dazzling technologies. This seems ironic since biblical scholarship remains a vital enterprise, but one conducted for a smaller (and increasingly more contentious) group of "elite" scholars for whom scripture makes no claim on their personal lives.

To refresh our preaching and worship, let's open the windows to our hearts and imaginations (and our Bibles), gather together in one place, and see what the Spirit may pour into our memories and imaginations. Let's explore the following ideas through the pages of this book:

1. Reading the Bible aloud can become sacramental, a means of grace.
2. There are many different kinds of ways to read scripture, and the different perspectives that arise from these ways revitalize our experience and understanding of biblical texts.
3. Biblical critical studies opened up multiple readings for me, but many of my companions on the journey of faith found that these same studies destroyed the sacramental quality of reading scripture—scripture became a "problem" that could not be solved.
4. The discipline of performance studies has helped to fuse together the best of these childhood experiences of scripture; it has enabled me to rediscover and reaffirm the quality of reading as a means of grace, and to renew my appreciation of the expanding discipline of biblical criticism.
5. Critical reading of scripture that takes into account its orality informs our interpretation for preaching, awakens the senses as it awakens the heart, and increases the capacity of scripture to engage both our imaginations and intellects held within the grace of God.

My hope is that anyone who reads this book and who dares to rise in the assembly of worshipers to read scripture aloud with intention, clarity of mind and voice, and expression or anyone who dares to preach more faithfully from them, will be refreshed by the Spirit of God, blowing across the pages. If we are so

renewed, perhaps we will discover what Larkin's speaker does at
the end of the poem–that the "accoutred frowsty barn" he has
visited is of great value:

> A serious house on serious earth it is,
> In whose blent air all our compulsions meet,
> Are recognized, and robed as destinies.
> And that much can never be obsolete,
> Since someone will forever be surprising
> A hunger in himself to be more serious,
> And gravitating with it to this ground,
> Which, he once heard, was proper to grow wise in,
> If only that so many dead lie round.[15]

CHAPTER 1

WHAT COMMUNICATION MEANS FOR PREACHING AND PROCLAMATION

To study communication is to examine the actual social process wherein significant symbolic forms are created, apprehended and used.

JAMES CAREY[1]

Communication is a word used so often that its sharp definitive edges are nearly worn away. In any given context, we might be talking about either equipment or essences, about language or instruments. Broadly speaking, the study of human communication is the study of message-making among human beings. No less than twenty-eight academic disciplines draw upon the study of human speaking! Scholars representing any one of these disciplines are likely to give a different account of what communication consists of, what its boundaries for research are, and what you are supposed to do with the research and knowledge once it is gathered. It's time to make clear how I would define it.

I like what Peter Hawkins says about communication. He imagines communication not so much as a discrete field of inquiry with clearly drawn disciplinary boundaries, but as the glue that holds education for ministry together. How can we say we are educated for the practice of ministry if we cannot translate what we have learned in the seminary into "good news" for others? Communication is a "process wherein what is privately held becomes common property."[2]

The preacher turns to the expressive arts of oral reading, recitation, and storytelling to help translate words on a page into living speech that invokes the Spirit of God. Encounters with God's Spirit become public by means of speech and enactment and thereby the "common property" of those gathered in Christ's name.

THE PREACHER AS COMMUNICATOR OF WORD AND PRESENCE

When a preacher stands alone to speak before a congregation, he or she is standing within an expanding swirl of ritual activity, a swirl that electronic technologies are turning into a rich integration of color, movement, space, music, and sound. What the preacher is there to do is to bear public witness to God's ongoing communication and self-disclosure through Jesus Christ, whom Christians take to be a Risen Sovereign and mediator of God's grace. As a form of human expressive speech, preaching itself can be viewed as oral, visual, and kinesthetic action; full of meaning; and a punctuation mark within a "sacred ceremony which draws persons together in fellowship and commonality."[3]

We can describe the sermon as a kind of oral *text* that a preacher embodies and enacts within a community's ritual performance of its corporate faith. James Carey tells us that "texts are not always printed on pages or chiseled in stone—though sometimes they are. Usually, they are texts of public utterance or shaped behavior."[4] The goal of preaching is to make the truth of God in Christ Jesus—as it is articulated, enacted, and embodied by the preacher—the *common property* of the worshiping community. The preacher does this by lending human voice, body, personality, intellect, and attitude to make the oral text visible, audible, intelligible, and evocative. *Preaching is "enfleshed" speech; it is a performed utterance. It is not the creation of a perfect oral form, nor is it simply the successful display of a "media-friendly" style. It is the embodiment through speech and gesture of a Word that God has entrusted to that preacher for a given occasion.* The preacher has a responsibility to speak in ways such that the Word of God can be heard and become "present" in the community.

There is an element of humility and simplicity in a preacher's readiness to speak–all that a preacher really has to work with is voice, body, thought, language, and sensitivity to culturally and liturgically prescribed conventions of speech. By the standards of our day, Jesus might well have been a poor speaker! He was not always clear in what he said, hardly ever comprehensible (especially to the rich and powerful who listened to his teachings), was certainly unpredictable, and therefore was not easily "packaged" for mass distribution.[5] However, by his presence Jesus disclosed a way of being and acting in the light and grace of God, making his listeners understand themselves and their situations differently.

"Being present" to God, to the congregation, and to the message itself presses a preacher beyond mere display of vocal technique; the mastery of technique is not enough to evoke the presence of the Holy. Efficiency does not necessarily mean efficacy. The one who preaches and who leads a congregation through the performance of liturgy, biblical text, and sermon does so in the presence of Christ and therefore does so with reverence, love, and humility. One cultivates a style for speaking and leadership by maintaining a life of prayerful presence before God, understanding the purpose and intentions of each act of worship, and becoming aware of the roles of posture, gesture, and eye contact in leading congregations through those acts of worship.

ORGANIZING IDEAS AND IMAGES FOR COMMUNICATION

Paul Soukup tells us that thinking about communication must be organized around images or analogues:

People tend to conceptualize communication in a certain way and organize their thinking around these images. Such thinking, of course, often conflicts with communication theorizing from a different perspective, one that chooses to favor a different image of the communication process.[6]

This is good news! No longer is our thinking about communication constrained by images and analogues such as I learned about in seminary. *Communication* was primarily concerned with efficiency and effect. In my experience as a theological student and then as a teacher in the seminary, *communication* exclusively described either the study and practice of a set of skills or techniques for public speaking or the use of media equipment.

The dominant image in communication studies for a long time was a "bow and arrow"; it pictured the process as follows:

- The speaker "discovers" an idea and begins to organize material.
- The speaker finds a recognizable form and begins to shape the message.
- The speaker employs devices that "illustrate" the discourse in order to enhance its effect and impact on the listener.
- The message is "delivered" in ways that make competent use of the speaker's character, command of voice, emotional expression, and gesture.

Using this model, we imagine a speaker holding a "bow" by which he or she sends the "arrow" of the message to the "target" of the listener. What any speaker needs to learn is how to "hit the mark" with the message. The "bow-and-arrow" model of communication suggests that in the preaching event "the archer's arrows carry God's Word to the target, with the effect of changing the listener's attitudes, beliefs or behaviors."[7]

This classical, conventional model of communication is certainly *a* way of thinking of preaching. But it is not the *only* way to imagine it. The process of preparing and speaking a sermon does not simply move along a one-way street between the text, the speaker, and the listener. Ronald Pelias puts it this way: "Meaning emerges in the act of communication, in the transactional process of the participants. It is not something one person gives another. Instead, people create meaning through dialogue, through talk. People construct meaning in the process of communication."[8] Fred

Craddock demonstrates the inadequacy of the bow-and-arrow model by showing us how texts "speak" in their own ways. A biblical text *does* something when it *says* something. It praises God, laments a loss, pleads on behalf of the poor, instructs a struggling church, tells a story of Jesus or one of Jesus' apostles, or dreams of both beginnings and endings.[9] Pelias' and Craddock's thinking about communication tells us that some dynamic, interactional and *incarnational* elements that are crucial to a *theological* understanding of communication are not adequately accounted for in a bow-and-arrow model. In order to preach from a text, the preacher has to first listen attentively to what a text is saying and how it is doing the talking in the preacher's imagination.[10]

The bow-and-arrow model, for all its limitations, does account for some desired effects and expectations for preaching. One of the crucial aims of the preacher is what Henry Mitchell has called "behavioral change." Preachers *want* their sermons to make a difference in the lives of their listeners; they want to *teach* as well as delight. The aim of any effective communication is the reduction of uncertainty. The preacher wants the gospel to be clearly presented so that the listener can make an informed response to its claims.

One preacher observed that when she graduated from seminary, the mainline Protestant pulpits were strangely silent when it came to the subjects of "conversion," "discipleship," or any other evidence of the "power God gives to implement changes in the...lives of others."[11] However we reimagine communication models, we do not want to lose sight of the ways that preaching becomes an occasion for behavioral change in the minds, hearts, and lives of listeners.

I also do not want to completely ignore matters of style and technique in the teaching of preaching as oral communication. In fact, in the next chapter I want to go through a process in which I worked with a preacher on these very matters. Any preacher would only benefit from training the voice and body to be more responsive to the thought and emotional life of the sermon the preacher has developed. Living and preaching in an electronic culture means that such subjects are still a part of our concern. However, our awareness of what "communicates" in the preaching moment has expanded beyond the preoccupation with the speaker's manual of vocal techniques and gestures. "It is not words...that count above all in communication, but what surrounds them: the whole environment, the atmosphere, the material conditions, the media employed, and everything that usually passes unnoticed."[12]

Those of us who teach preaching from this widening angle of vision need to be clear about what relationships within a kaleidoscopic array we are focusing on. We want an analogue for communication that widens our interpretative lens beyond the technical training of the preacher's voice and body and deepens our gaze on the full scope of a preacher's process of preparation and delivery. We want an analogue that does not simply focus on that moment when the preacher opens his or her mouth in the pulpit, but helps us to understand the theological implications of preaching: Why does a preacher say anything at all? Communication cannot strictly be imagined as a straight classical line that moves from sermon idea, through illustrations and "proofs," and finally to a passive listener. The shape of the communicative event is more kaleidoscopic; it looks more like a web of relationships between a variety of speakers and listeners than like a bow and arrow. The feel of it is more dramatic than discursive. For these reasons, I am working from a perspective drawn from performance studies to develop an image of preaching as "dramatic" communication.

THE DRAMATIC CHARACTER OF HUMAN COMMUNICATION

A "dramatic" perspective within communication assumes that "people fundamentally are performing creatures who engage in an ongoing process of giving speech to their thoughts and feelings. Through the act of performing, people make their lives meaningful and define themselves."[13] All forms of human speech are *potentially* aesthetic, depending on how the speaker intends communication, what the definition of "art" is in a particular culture, and how it is received by an audience.

For example, imagine the following scene. Two lovers are sitting across a table from each other at a sidewalk café. They have learned from their culture some appropriate (and inappropriate) ways of speaking to each other, responding with voice and body, maintaining a measure of distance or closing that measure of distance between them, and being aware that they are not only each other's "audience" but that other "audiences" are present as well. This is an example of "performance in everyday life" by which the sexual drives of human beings are focused and shaped in ways that are sanctioned by their culture. Each expects from the other certain behaviors as the performance unfolds—a look from the eyes, a tender movement of the hand, a certain vocal tone.

Now take this same scene and put it into a play or a movie. What is inherently "aesthetic" about human behavior becomes framed by the same culture as "art." The artistic form will not violate the performance expectations of lovers in everyday life, but will heighten and deepen those conventions in a way that draws the audience into identifying with the performance of "love." So it is with preaching. An announcement of the good news of Jesus Christ arises out of the same "stuff" of life: a plenitude of performances in everyday life in which the preacher is participant and audience. Attending a child's birthday party, participating in a march or demonstration, reading a biblical text in the quiet of one's own study, or reading a bedtime story to one's son or daughter are all cultural performances that display aesthetic impulses. When a preacher identifies the embodied truth of these ordinary scenes, then heightens and deepens the meaning of these scenes through the arts of preaching, a congregation identifies with the truth that is embodied and performed by the preacher.

A *dramatistic* perspective in the study of human communication does not wish to restrict our understanding of communicative behaviors (from the pulpit or elsewhere) to their discursive or logical contents. Art and other products and processes of the imagination come into range from this angle, as well as "the more existential aspects of communication, raising questions of self-understanding and identity through expression."[14] Aesthetic images of communication, specifically those grounded in the study of human behavior as *performance,* help us to lay the foundation of both a theological approach to communication with a strategy for teaching preaching as human communication, and a performance approach within the study of human communication as a drama of interaction.

First, we learn from this approach that any *intentional* transaction between human beings is "dramatic." Embedded in this claim is the idea that all human communication possesses what are called dramatistic features: a speaker or speakers saying particular things in a particular manner for a particular reason in a particular time and place to a particular audience.[15] Dramatism opens up a way of thinking theologically about communication. Human beings become actualized in and through encounters. God is among the infinite array of "others" we encounter as we go about being human. In fact and belief, Christians imagine God to be a Holy One who initiates encounters with us through such historical and mythic events as Creation and Incarnation. We believe, for example, that God has particularly disclosed God's Self in humanity's encounter with Jesus of Nazareth, who was then taken by the church to be God's Christ.

By casting the entire field of human relations as dramatic, dramatism considerably expands our imagination regarding speakers, texts, and listeners. Human social and personal life in all its complexity and richness can be defined in dramatistic terms, and such interactions are potentially *aesthetic.*

Too often, however, our talk about drama and preaching is burdened by a strained comparison of the preacher to the stage actor. Even though actors and preachers share "word-made-flesh" as a central metaphor for their art and theology respectively, preachers are usually suspicious when the term *actor* surfaces in their talk about preaching. Sometimes *acting* is used descriptively. In the preacher's vocabulary it refers to a constellation of all that is "theatrical" about preaching. The actor in the preacher's imagination is a stand-in for any cultural performer of literary texts who realizes intentionality in artistic, literary texts through voice, gesture, movement, and/or impersonation.

More often the word is used pejoratively by preachers. For them, *to act* means to exhibit the kind of flashy, stylistic techniques that help to "embalm the sermon and put it on view."[16] This anti-theatrical prejudice has deep, historic roots.[17] Some contemporary homileticians quickly dismiss "pulpit theater" as a stand-in for *real* preaching. David Buttrick warns that the dramatic monologue in pulpit performance edges out the "mystery of God-With-Us" and replaces it with "psychologies of faith."[18] Elizabeth Achtemeier dismisses pulpit theater as a kind of "experimental" preaching that "abandons the biblical message altogether and becomes nothing more than artistic or symbolic performance, open to a wide variety of meanings." Dramatic monologues are not, she declares, "adequate substitutes for the proclamation of the biblical Word."[19]

Nevertheless, preachers who follow the impulse to actually become actors in pulpit theater stand on firm, traditional ground. Quintilian turned the orators' attention to actors, claiming that impersonation might enable them to "display inner thoughts of adversaries, introduce conversations, bring down gods from heaven, raise the dead, or give voice to entire cities and peoples."[20] Actors, then as now, have much to teach speakers. Haddon Robinson says it well, "While a preacher is more than an actor, [he or she] should not be less."[21]

The appearance of a number of books of dramatic monologues suggests there is a new appetite for the dramatic form as a means of proclamation, especially in so-called "seeker" churches. There is also a rising number of "Christian" theater groups.[22] A healthy regard for the integrity of the dramatic form surfaces anew, exhibiting an appreciation for the kind of union between action and word that worshipers seek in their communal practice of Word and Sacrament. Worship itself is "dramatic," because it arises out of a "religious" human impulse to *act together,* that is, "to do something that either changes the relationship to the Divine or expresses it."[23] I certainly do not want to discourage preachers from exploring these opportunities. Yet I do not want to leave the impression that donning a wig, beard, and robe in order to adopt the persona of a biblical character makes preaching dramatic. Nor do I want to say that "being dramatic" simply describes a wide range of stylistic elements, such as heightened vocal acrobatics and extravagant gesticulation. We can get more work out of this word *drama* than this. Drama can also be pressed into service as a hermeneutical device for interpreting the meaning of the preaching event; it can also tell us something about the character of preaching itself.

THE DRAMATIC CHARACTER OF PREACHING

One day after a preaching class a student in the class asked me, "Can you tell me something? Isn't preaching a lot like acting?" Her voice was muted, her tone was conspiratorial, as if she was probing a dark secret. Further conversation revealed that before she attended seminary and then entered the ministry, this student had been an actress. Now she was trying to find her way into the study of preaching by drawing some analogies between the expressive arts of acting and preaching.

This is a familiar scene in the preaching classroom. Students often appear who have loyalties to two life worlds–to religion on the one hand and to a particular art world on the other. Students who have an affinity for the theatrical arts seem to have a more difficult time integrating their faith with their chosen art because of the dense, ambiguous, and often contentious relationship that has existed between church and theater throughout the development of Western culture. These students work out the competing loyalties in various ways. Some enter the world of theater on its own terms and attempt to live out their faith perspective. Some join with others with similar faith commitments to produce theater. And still others are like this student, and their interest in drama awakens the possibility that skills and techniques that the actor employs will help them discover how to preach. What instructions would I give this student on how to build a bridge between these two forms of speech? Is it simply a matter of writing and performing monologues on an occasional Sunday or for special liturgical celebrations? Or is there more to it than that?

What is *essentially* dramatic about the character of preaching? If a preacher has the time, talent, and training, he or she would do well to study dramatic form by reading and watching plays. Preachers have a lot to learn from those who have developed the skills for characterization. Playwrights are keen observers of humanity. They pay attention to the details of human appearance and behavior and place a set of characters into situations to explore how those characters respond and change. To watch a playwright's characters work through toward resolution the conflicts they face is to put ourselves in their position and wonder what would we do if we had to make the same choices. This is instructive for the preacher. "To study drama," wrote E. Winston Jones, "is to study the highest of the art forms for influencing character." Since it takes as its subject the "reproduction of human living" and makes primary appeals to feelings and emotions, drama enables vicarious participation in various types of situations and allows us to "live through them."[24] This is one reason why some churches are making fuller use of short plays in their ministry of proclamation.

Some preachers make use of the dramatic form by developing sermons in the form of monologues. To learn how to create, develop, and perform a biblical character is to learn a valuable homiletical skill. By speaking "as if" a preacher is from the supposed world of a biblical text, he or she involves a listener in a psychological drama unfolding in a biblical character's interiority. However, not every preacher has the level of skill, training, or even inclination to take on this kind of preaching. Every preacher, however, has the capacity to do the following:

- See, hear, and feel the "truth" of performances in everyday life
- Give thought, form, and structure to that truth by finding the language and form of a sermon
- Let the forms and structures of that sermon "come through" the body, voice, and personality of the preacher in the performance of a sermon
- Lead a congregation to identify with the embodied truth as found, spoken, and enacted in sermon performance

In this sense, preachers share a kinship with actors on the stage of the theater. Preachers are "ritual actors," that is, they play an assigned role in the performance of liturgy when they enact a sermon. Like the actor in the theater, the preacher as ritual actor strives for *congruity* between action suited to the word and the word to the action. An actor in the theater is deemed "truthful" when he or she is able to make this congruity happen. In preaching, "truth-telling" has a grander dimension. What we hope for when we preach are moments where we are visited by the Word Incarnate, places where flesh and spirit have somehow become as one, holy places where we behold the Presence of "Word-Among-Us."

Preaching is "dramatic" because a preacher uses language, voice, body, and imagination to set words and worlds on a collision course toward one another. Dramatic preaching "tells the truth" when it becomes a strategy of grace (not a display of skill) and a way to "communicate the gospel of their culture with as much wit and skill, passion and ingenuity, as possible."[25] The processes involved in preparing to speak sermons is fraught with suspense, because preaching is a search both for a language of lived experience AND for a way of speaking that is believable at a time when coherent theological frameworks have collapsed.

Preaching a sermon is a drama that unfolds in several contexts at once. First, it unfolds within the historical context of a "great cloud of witnesses," that is, in relationship to all of those who speak (and have spoken) as Christian preachers. Second, it unfolds within the context of the speaker's own human existence in relation to other statements of faith collected as "Christian theology." And, finally, it unfolds temporally as a public utterance within the performance of liturgy.

THE PREACHER AS "HOLY" PERFORMER: THE DRAMATIC CHARACTER OF RITUAL

Preachers will not be able to escape their roles as ritual performers. From this perspective, the preacher realizes that the speaking event that he or she is staging is not an end in itself. "A sermon belongs to ritual and shares in its ambiguities."[26] What is dramatic about Christian liturgical performance is the pull of *this* (an order of worship) against *that* (the structures of everyday life) in a way that opens up "holes in the fabric of things, through which life-giving power flows into the world."[27] Preaching the sermon is an action, a "doing of the Word," and in it, the preacher "acts" with an eye toward fullness; that is, the completion of the performed, embodied sermon. Performance is first an act that *makes* the sermon. Performing it as a liturgical act, however, is an act that *breaks* it. Preaching is the creation of a finite form (sermon) that is brought to the assembly in order to be broken by a holy God who is radically other than festival, ceremony, or even ritual performance.

The preacher, as an actor in a holy ritual, seeks the emptiness of "holes" that liturgical performance opens up. The pull toward *this* (the embodiment of the preacher's own words) against *that* (the creation of empty space in liturgical structures) is a necessary dynamic in the new poetics of preaching. Without the theatricality of the performed speaker's drama, we have liturgy performed poorly. Without an awareness of its location in ritual performance, we veer dangerously toward "entertainment with too little efficacy."[28]

Actors become efficacious teaching partners in homiletics as figures of both holiness and poverty in human aesthetic communication. Actors from Peter Brook's "holy" theater ask, "Can the invisible be made visible through the performer's presence?"[29] The central paradox of Christian liturgy is that it uses ordinary things (bread, wine, books, cloth, fire, and water) to speak of the Holy. The preacher becomes radically present in the assembly as a "holy" actor when he or she stages the speaker's drama of the sermon as an "ordinary" thing–that is, as an aesthetic object that finds completeness in performance, but that is brought into the liturgical frame in order to be broken by a "language of actions, a language of sounds."[30] It is in *this* breaking that a Divine Presence acts and is therefore known in the "holy theater" of liturgical performance.

What kinds of competencies are required to participate in this drama of preaching? I want to address these matters in forthcoming chapters. In the next chapter we will walk through a process by which one preacher and I worked through matters of style and technique to some deeper issues of embodiment and enactment in proclamation.

WORKSHOP 1: PUBLIC READING AS A COMMUNICATIVE ACT

Three workshops are interspersed between the chapters of this book. Each one is designed to help the public reader establish some learning goals and learn some competencies for the public reading of scripture. The workshops each take a different point of emphasis: (1) the public reader *as an oral communicator;* (2) the text *as the subject of study;* and (3) the *meaning of the event itself as a communicative act* within the performance of liturgy. All three workshops aim to enrich the capacity of readers and listeners to attend to the Word of God as it addresses us in the spoken text.

This first workshop focuses on the relationship between the reader and the listeners, using a traditional model of communication. The reader is imagined as a "messenger," the text to be read as the "message," and the listener as the "receptor." When a reader first reads a text, that text will certainly have some kind of impact on the reader. It will challenge, move, perplex, or persuade. It will certainly beg for the interpretations that must arise out of the reader's own questions.

What does this text *say?* What words, phrases, and structures of thought are employed to get it said? What is the relationship between this text and the literary context that it comes from? Who is this text speaking *to?* What can we know about the first listeners of this text? Does the text provide any clues to the relationship that the author has with those that the author is addressing?

How does this text *feel?* There is the presence of an author or authors here. What is the authorial attitude toward the things being described? What words provide the clues to the authorial attitude or perspective? How does this text *mean? Meaning* is the complex of thought, authorial intent and perspective, use of language, phrasing, and word choice that may be bodied forth in the act of public reading.

The reader lends embodied meaning to the text by transforming it from silent print into a form of speech. To do so, the reader of the text is concerned with conveying what the text means by focusing voice and body for the task. Of course, the reader understands that the performance of this text is not meant to be exhaustive of all the potential meanings. What the reader does hope to do is convey through word choice, vocal emphasis, and inflection his or her best apprehension of authorial motive, emotional attitude, and thought.

One thing to make clear is that this form of communication is not acting, that is, the reader does not intend to embody or impersonate the authorial presence in any way. The reader relies on a style best described by the term *suggestion.* Through the expressive use of voice and gesture, the reader recreates his or her own experience of being addressed by the text so that the text can "speak" in the assembly.

From this angle of vision, public reading is analogous to public speaking, another familiar form of cultural performance. Although the reader is not inventing his or her own words, the reader serves as the channel for someone else's words to reach an audience. This is not to suggest that public reading is not creative. What you are doing is taking a set of symbols that are silently arranged on the page and creating new dimensions of meaning by speaking them. To reach the audience with the richness of the text, the reader must take care to appropriately introduce it; convey it with expression, empathy, and concentration; and hold the audience's attention.

FOR PRACTICE

1. Once you have selected a text, read it aloud to yourself to become acquainted with how it sounds when read. (For the purpose of this exercise, let's select 1 Corinthians 12:4–11).

2. Does a pattern emerge from the phrasing of the text? Is there a rhythm? (Note the pattern in verses 8 and following. "To one and to another.") See if you can capture the rhythm of the phrasing as you sound out the text.

3. What exactly is the writer saying? Can you put the author's thoughts into your own words? Identify what parts of the author's thoughts are not clear to you. What words capture the author's thought the best? Place emphasis on those words when you read them.

4. As you read the text aloud, can you get some clues about how the author feels? What is the author trying to do? Explain? Persuade? Give an illustration of a point? Tell a story? Thought, motive, and attitude appear together in human communication.

5. As you read, what begins to happen to your voice? How does your body want to get into the act? Do you find yourself wanting to establish eye contact with your listener? If your liturgical convention allows for that to happen, learn parts of your passage well enough to establish eye contact, then return to the page (if you need to). Throughout your rehearsal process you should begin to feel more comfortable as a "stand-in" for the author, suggesting the author's presence through your own voice, thought, attitude, and body.

CHAPTER 2

SPEAKING AND HEARING A "LIVELY WORD"

In midwinter, St. Francis is calling out to an almond tree, "Speak to me of God!" and the almond tree breaks into bloom. It comes alive. There is no other way of witnessing to God but by aliveness.

BROTHER DAVID STENDL-RAST, O.S.B[1]

My friend was waiting to see me in my office, and I was late getting out of class. She was a busy pastor of a church in the area and had asked for an appointment to talk about sermon delivery. What exercises or disciplines could she practice to enliven or animate her pulpit speech? As I hurried to our meeting, I mused on how often it is that preachers ask for help with this part of their preaching.

I am not surprised that preachers are looking for ways to enliven their speech. We inhabit an increasingly electronic culture in which an array of speakers barrage us with messages delivered in a highly charged, animated style. The temptation for preachers is to become overly pragmatic by simply focusing on speaking technique at the expense of deeper issues of embodiment. "Aliveness" is not the same thing as enjoying the lively presence of God in worship, Word, and Sacrament. "God-with-us" means that we are "with" those to whom we speak in the presence of God. A speaking image transmitted by means of radio or television is disembodied. No matter how energetic or animated the image is, we cannot enter into an embodied relationship with it. Placing our voices and bodies into service of the Word in worship means being present to the Word as it works itself out in our minds and hearts. In this chapter I hope to place vocal and physical work in the context of the prayerful work a preacher must do.

MOVING FROM TECHNIQUE TO EMBODIED WITNESS: AN EXPLORATION

Some preachers are fortunate enough to receive formal instruction in sermon delivery in theological education. They are privileged to have courses offered that specifically focus on the use of voice and body in presenting their sermons. Few theological schools make this kind of training a high priority, however, and too often, the entire matter of voice production and even delivery is marginalized. Consequently, ministers are usually left to their own resources and initiatives. My friend was one such person; she had done very little work on sermon delivery in seminary and was waiting to see what suggestions I might give her on this important aspect of her preaching.

When I finally arrived at the meeting, my friend and I started talking together at the point of her concern—the use of voice and body during the preaching event. We discussed how difficult it is for a busy pastor to make room in his or her life for this kind of special training. The entire matter of vocal control and voice production is best handled by a competent instructor, a specialist who can lead the student through sets of exercises that will help make the preacher's voice and body more responsive to the thought-worlds of scripture, the listening congregation, and even the sermon itself.[2] If such a coach is too difficult to find, then some excellent resources are available in print, if the preacher is motivated to work through the exercises on her own.[3]

The two of us established a learning covenant that would help to focus her efforts first on vocal production, then on the expressive use of the body. First, we would begin working to cultivate some awareness that would help her improve her use of voice. After that, I would lead her through some exercises that would focus on the scriptures she selected for her preaching and reading aloud. We would treat the scripture not simply as a text fixed on a page but as an *experience to be shared* with her listeners. The aim for our work was to help her voice and body to become more responsive to the thoughts and emotions she wished to express in her sermons and also to the experiences of God as mediated through scripture.

DISCOVERING THE SERMON AS ORAL EVENT

Anyone who speaks in public knows that he or she has certain strengths and areas for improvement in the use of the voice. The first task is to identify what those specific areas are. In my friend's case, we noted that she had many strengths of vocal expression. Her voice was bright, audible, and clear, especially when she used a microphone. We listened to some tapes of her sermons and noted that she had a tendency to drop the voice at the end of her sentences. Some of those sentences seemed too long, and the thoughts she wished to express quite difficult to follow.

This is a common problem for those who use a manuscript for preaching. I suggested to her what I have suggested to others, that they begin working away from strict dependence on the manuscript and learn to write in an oral style. When a preacher is tied to the manuscript, it is difficult to develop the vocal dynamics that are appropriate for oral communication. We tend to look more at the manuscript than we do our listener, making it very difficult to establish and maintain eye contact. The only parts of our body that we need to involve in communication are the head and hands. What a contrast to other forms of speaking. In conversation with friends, for example, see how much more of your body is involved in telling a personal story or a joke, in describing someone or something, or in competing with others to make a point. See how alive and expressive the voice and body can be!

When the preacher is tied to a manuscript, however, much of the body shuts down, particularly if it is behind a pulpit. The voice is trained to follow the demands of reading long sentences, not the spontaneous rhythms of conversational speech. Paragraphs and punctuation give a silent reader clues for response, but do little or nothing for the hearer. If a speaker focuses primarily on following the flow of written sentences, the kind of vocal qualities that animate lively conversation are lost.

I suggested that my friend begin with one of Clyde Fant's principles—that she speak the sermon first, then write it down. After studying a text carefully, the preacher discovers some main thoughts and directions he or she wants to pursue. Then comes a process of "talking out" a draft of the sermon to determine what the thought, movement, and direction of the sermon will be. The preacher writes out an "oral manuscript" that will eventually be the basis for the sermon event.

By speaking the sermon into consciousness, the preacher will find pieces or blocks that she knows by heart. It could be a deep conviction, a cherished memory, or a vivid image. A series of statements or a topic of concern might naturally arise out of the preacher's encounter with a biblical text, a lived situation, or a problem in the community. Turning these initial impressions into speech takes us a long way to what we want to say in the developing sermon. Fant shows how *writing* will then serve the *speaking* rather than the other way around.[4]

When one starts to speak the sermon as part of the process of preparing it for preaching, one becomes more aware of the body and its potential to express the sermon. My friend and I started to address the matter of gesture and other uses of the body in preaching. I experienced her as a very energetic speaker who frequently used her body to emphasize certain points or images. Her tendency was to punctuate what she was saying by using her hands or arms. There were even some places where she would underscore her message by walking to-and-fro from behind or beside the pulpit. By watching her on videotape, we were able to see that many of her movements, while animated and emphatic, were actually unfocused expressions of kinesthetic energy. What other choices might she make to speak with more expression and focus?

Don Wardlaw points out that there are at least two kinds of gestures: *emphatic* and *descriptive*.[5] In addition to being used to "make a point," the body can also be used to "make pictures." When a preacher "sees" again an image in his or her own mind's eye and selects appropriate descriptive language to recreate it in the listener's imagination, the body naturally follows the effort to help create that image.

For example, my friend was working on an excerpt from a sermon based on Psalm 127, focusing on the first two verses:

> Unless the LORD builds the house, those who build it labor in vain. Unless the LORD guards the city, the guard keeps watch in vain. It is in vain that you rise up early and go late to rest, eating the bread of anxious toil, for (God) gives sleep to (God's) beloved.

She was giving an account of her personal experience of working on a building project during a mission trip. One phrase that emerged from her story was this: "I came up to the site where we were to build the house. Some other crew members had already delivered the materials—the piles of cut lumber, buckets of nails, sheets of plywood—and I wondered, 'How will all of this turn into a place where someone can live?'"

At first she spoke this phrase as if she were giving a report. Her hands were clasped in front of her. She was making good eye contact and looked poised and balanced. Yet the entire experience for me changed when I asked her to *tell me with her body* where the materials were. At that point, the word picture became much clearer. She "showed" me specific places where the materials were located in her imagination—lumber there in a tall pile, buckets of nails over there, plywood to the right. It was a good example of how the body naturally will conjoin language and gesture to create images in the preaching event.

DISCOVERING PREACHING AS EMBODIED PROCLAMATION

We worked in this way for several weeks and then, during one of our final sessions together, our conversation started taking a different turn. It seemed to us that our explorations of technique were leading us to some grander, more expansive matters. This preacher's concern with how she would develop her voice and body for preaching was certainly an important aspect of the ministry of proclamation. This is usually a way in which a labyrinth of communication issues opens up to *any* preacher. One's body and one's voice and how these are used in the preaching ministry are intensely *personal* issues. If you don't believe that, think about how you squirm when you hear yourself on tape or review a videotape of your preaching from the pulpit. I know some prominent and well-known preachers who are so uncomfortable about seeing themselves on videotape that they simply refuse to watch. The use of body and voice are so personal because one's body and voice are vitally connected to one's sense of identity and selfhood. Body and voice are ways of expressing, but they are also means of knowing. When one is preaching, one is "thinking" with the body. What the body does in the act of preaching (as in conversation) is in accord with what it thinks and knows.

"How the body thinks and knows" is an issue that is quite current in religious studies of all sorts. Scholars are asking what the contribution of the body is to the task of making sense of experience and of interpreting reality. Those who want to understand how the body "knows" or "thinks" often go to those enactments and embodiments that take place in communal performances of roles and rituals. Communities embody and enact their primary commitments and convictions by means of performance.

Preaching, for example, takes place in the context of worship, a community's ensemble performance of praise, petition, and commissioning. Preaching is also the solo performance of a sermon, a minister's enactment of her professional role and an enactment of that minister's interpretation of God's word to a congregation on a specific occasion. Rebecca Chopp might say that preaching and the communal worship of God is "saving work, a practice that...offers a material vision and an embodied wisdom" that a community expresses as performance.[6]

PUBLIC READING AND PROCLAMATION: A TIE THAT BINDS

Within the structure of liturgy, the act of preaching is connected to the public reading and presentation of biblical texts. One of the things I want to accent in this book is the relationship between the oral presentation and performance of texts and the oral performance of the sermon. How might the pastor's oral study and performance of a given text enliven his or her performance of a sermon? Or if the pastor will not be serving in the role of "reader" for the day, how can he or she prepare the reader for the kind of performance that will open up the hearts and minds of all who will hear the sermon? The preacher's work is so much easier if a text has been rendered in an evocative way.

The public reading of a text is not simply conducted to inform the listener of the words that are lying on the page of some Bible. We are so caught and constrained by certain habits and traditions of communicating scripture that I have often wondered why we even bother to have the text read aloud at all! Since it is more often than not done poorly, I would almost rather have the opportunity to read the text for myself in silence, or at least have the congregation read it together, than to have someone attempt it who does not understand either the text or the importance of reading it aloud in worship. The public, oral presentation of a text within the performance of worship is an interpretation both of that text and of the importance of its place in the ensemble performance of worship. One of the themes we will explore in this book is oral interpretation of scripture as a resource for preaching. The way that "reading" is done says a lot about how valuable the presence of the biblical text is to that community and to the sermon that reflects on it.

Training the voice and body to become more responsive to the language, thought, attitudes, and intentions we find in biblical texts will improve the way that we choose to present them in worship. It also trains us to respond more fully (and become more available) to the expressions, interpretations, and perceptions presented by our own sermons. The disciplines of oral reading, recitation, and retelling stories from scripture will help to train the voice and body to "see" the text with new eyes and hear it with new ears. They can also teach our voices and bodies to "think" in ways that will enable our own sermons to come alive in the hearing and imaginations of our listeners.

"Body thinking" in the study and enactment of biblical literature increases our degree of investment and participation in the "world" of the texts we select for preaching and invites the congregation to more fully participate in worship through listening to the texts. We must never overlook the importance of vocal and physical training to the act of preaching. However, there are other ways of "training" our eyes and ears for preaching. Hans-Ruedi Weber tells us that learning how to approach and enter the world that a biblical text creates "will shape the right timbre and appropriate loudness or quietness of the voice. It will dictate the moments of speed, slowness or silence" and help the speaker to "find the right look in the eye and the right gestures" when we speak about them.[7]

We often note the value of the formal study of public speaking in preparing for our preaching ministries. Analogies between these two forms of speech–public speaking and preaching–are not so difficult to draw. What I want to tease out is how other forms of public address–oral interpretation and recitation of literature, for example–and a study of communication generated by the new and evolving discipline of performance studies deepens and enriches our practice of preaching.

It is easy to become so focused on how we speak that we start to forget why we speak at all. It is my conviction that how we speak is intimately related to why. "Technique" is often how conversations about "delivery" might start; it might be the first site we visit in order to renew our preaching. It is by no means the end of the journey. We live in a culture that places an extraordinarily high value on hype. Those of us who serve God through the church too easily fall under the spell of techniques and manipulation and lose our grounding in theology.

WHY WE SPEAK OF THE HOLY

A group of clergy and laity in my own denomination (the United Church of Christ) once observed that "forces today that contest our loyalty to Jesus Christ [include] techniques of management and manipulation that have elbowed aside biblical preaching, sound theological teaching, living worship and sacrament."[8] Evans Crawford recently amplified this theme in *The Hum: Call and Response in African-American Preaching,* writing that the ground for preaching these days is neither a technique for speaking "properly" nor one for deriving ideas from biblical texts. "It is nothing less than the quality of the preacher's relationship to God as revealed in Jesus Christ."[9]

When preachers such as my friend or other students of preaching come to me with questions about improving technique,

I first take that concern at face value. I begin with these matters as best I can in the limited time that is usually available. I will then examine with them how oral approaches to the study and public performance of texts teaches them to become more responsive in their own processes of preparing and speaking their sermons. Yet I wonder whether what they are groping for is what Alan Jones identified in *Sacrifice and Delight:* "Leadership in the church is not so much a matter of acquiring skills as developing a centered spirituality of presence."[10] Preachers who want to work on improving the use of their voices and bodies in the performance of their sermons, or even in their oral presentation of texts, are probably not deeply invested in putting a stylistic, delicate gloss over their sermon production. Strip away questions of technique and what you expose is a concern with authenticity, "centeredness," and a "spirituality of presence." My friend's initial interrogations into the mechanics of her own preaching were inviting us both into deeper waters, that space that H. E. Luccock once called "the soul of delivery."[11]

If (like Paul) I am "preaching Christ and him crucified" and "Christ in you the hope of glory," I need to know who Jesus Christ is *today* and how to maintain a vital relationship to Him. Preaching should be a manner of speaking and being present in ways that draw people toward Christ. The preacher does not speak from within a community of faith in order to disclose some private arena of experience, reveal some secret knowledge, or reach the summit of privileged information. Nor does the authentic preacher want to dazzle and delight a bored audience. The reason we work at our preaching is to more faithfully and authentically give our best understanding of who Jesus Christ is, how our relationship with Him can be deepened and expanded, and how that relationship is grounded in a history of God's dealings with a people with whom God has established a covenant.

As our time of learning was coming to an end, my friend helped to place this matter of preaching technique into perspective. She handed me a copy of a poem she had been reading and asked if I knew it. I recognized the title, "Sunday Morning," by Wallace Stevens. The speaker in the poem observes a woman sitting alone, late on a Sunday morning, with the smell of coffee and oranges in the air. Dreaming a little, the poem's speaker notes, she feels "the dark encroachment of that old catastrophe [the crucifixion?]" and on "dreaming feet" passes "over the seas, to silent Palestine, dominion of the blood and sepulchre." My preacher friend had underlined that part of the poem, and she asked, "This is what we do every Sunday morning, isn't it? We make our way to the 'dominion of blood and sepulchre' to see if the rumors, the rumors of resurrection, are still true?"

These kinds of questions will take us beneath the gloss and glitter into the "soul" of delivery; it is the reason why we dare to speak of the Holy. We preach because we share a hunger for the Holy with those who dare to come and listen to us—we hunger for a God who gives grace in abundance, and we have tasted of that grace in the preaching event. We preach because we recognize our own poverty of spirit in the presence of this Holy God. We do not speak simply because we are gifted in the ways admired by a culture that is wired for sound and spectacle; we may even preach in spite of the fact that we are NOT gifted in those ways! We preach because we believe that something once happened in that "dominion of blood and sepulchre" and that it goes on happening in our personal and communal stories. It is that ineffable "something" that we call "Word." The Word prompts us to shape that living collection of stories, interpretations, and experiences in forms of public reading and address and learn to speak them with the energy and expressiveness that arise out of conviction, not "hype."

A second order of questions remain: What are those skills, habits, disciplines, and practices that help a preacher cultivate a "spirituality of presence" in the pulpit? These are questions that take us right to the central concerns of this book:

- A preacher can deepen or enhance his or her presence for the ministry of proclamation by attending in the study as well as in the pulpit to the oral/aural qualities of the scriptures used as texts for sermons.
- Reading aloud to oneself or to another better enables the preacher to be "addressed" by the Holy Spirit of God through the words of the many voices (those that are recorded as well as those that are *silenced* in the text).

- The *effect* of these words (emotionally, intellectually, theologically) gives shape and form to the preacher's own imagination and strategy for speaking the sermon.

These insights are from old traditions for speaking, but they have resonance suitable for speaking in our times. Jesus once spoke a parable that compared the scribe trained for the Realm of God to the "master of a household who brings out of his treasure what is new and what is old" (Mt. 13:52). Preachers are among the "scribes" of our day, and Jesus' comparison still resonates with us. Preaching is the act of bringing out the treasure of God's gospel of Jesus Christ. We live in the wake of a transformation of the Word. Our homiletical imaginations have been expanded to include more evocative presentations of biblical texts, themes, and stories in support of our preaching and worship. In the next three chapters we will learn how "three Rs"–reading, reciting, retelling–can help us cultivate a spirituality of being present both to God's Spirit, who addresses us through the scriptures, and to those who await what we shall say.

Workshop 2: Public Reading as an Interpretive Act

When a reader prepares a text for reading aloud, he or she is preparing to offer an interpretation of that text through the medium of speech. The reader does not intend that his or her oral interpretation exhaust all possibilities of ways the text might be read aloud. In fact, part of what keeps this manner of interpretation fresh is that each public reading belongs to the context and occasion for the reading. Each event of oral reading is different from any other; the evanescence of the oral event contributes to the richness of the text's possibilities for interpretation and incites interest and further study.

The one who is preparing a text for reading aloud is also joining the company of those who seek to increase their knowledge of what the text means. To accept responsibility for reading the text aloud is to open oneself up to new kinds of questions for study. For example, in the case of Jesus' encounter with the Syrophoenician woman in Mark 7, how do you think Jesus *sounded* when he spoke to the woman? How did she *sound* when she responded? Think of the different possibilities that present themselves when you ask that one question. How Jesus or the woman sounded is not crucial to a silent reading. If I were reading this text aloud, I would have to make some kind of choice as to how I would sound Jesus' controversial words, "It is not fair to take the children's food and throw it to the dogs." Before I could make an informed choice, I would have to know what other interpreters have said about the significance of this encounter in Mark's gospel. That problem of "oral" interpretation opens up a line of interrogation that Mark wants all the readers to engage in— *Who* is Jesus? What is happening to him in this story? *Who* is the Syrophoenician woman? What is the meaning of this encounter in Mark's overall presentation of his gospel?

The project of preparing to speak the text aloud either in worship, in the context of one's own sermon, or in some kind of Bible study means having to come to terms with the text on a different basis than that afforded by silent reading. You have to ask the same kinds of critical questions, but with a different twist if you are going to read it aloud. The idea is to become a "critic" more than a "performer." Your interest is in understanding as much as you can about the text in order to communicate its emerging set of meanings. Your voice and body are employed as hermeneutical tools.

I remember that once when I was conducting a study of the Syrophoenician woman, my entire experience and understanding of the text changed when I physically assumed the role of the woman. In accordance with the "stage directions" given by the narrator, I "came and fell down at his feet." I realized that I had very little *bodily* memory of being in this kind of subservient role. As a white, North American male, I never had to "fall down" before anyone! By assuming the posture suggested by the story, I came to understand the perspective of others throughout time and history who have been oppressed by stronger and more authoritative figures.

I went on to think of what it felt like to speak from this position. How humiliating it was! How embarrassing! And how necessary it has been for so many others in countless situations to have to adopt this position for speaking. When I listened to Jesus' response, "It is not fair to take the children's food and throw it to the dogs!" I felt feelings of hurt and outrage. You might have another kind of emotional reaction, but I doubt if it would be "spiritual." It would be a real and complex response to a predicament. I found it empowering to have her words to say, "Even the dogs under the table eat the children's crumbs."

To take seriously the possibilities afforded by using the voice and body as interpretive tools is to change the relationship we have to scripture. It offers up some concrete, visceral means of formulating the effect that scripture has on us as readers. It also opens up new questions for analysis and new vistas for understanding. It is a way of *enacting* the gestures, *embodying* the speakers, and following a path "into" the human predicaments presented in these situations.

FOR PRACTICE

1. Read Acts 2:1–4 several times.
2. Place yourself in the narrator's position. What is the narrator describing? What words or phrases create the impact that the narrator seeks to have on the listener? Underscore those

words or phrases and then place vocal and physical emphasis on these highlighted words.

3. Now place yourself in the situation of one of those "gathered together in one place." Read the text as if what it describes is actually happening in the moment, to you. Of course you won't literally "enact" the speaking in tongues. You are not attempting to impersonate the speaker, only to suggest the size, scope, and range of an enormous experience using the words you have available in the story. You are allowing the words you have been given lead you into the experience. How does this affect your reading?

4. Use your reading to recreate an experience you have had of utter and unexpected excitement. Let the memory of that experience inform your reading of the experience of the Spirit's outpouring. Have you ever been so excited about something that has happened that your enthusiasm "breaks free" from the constraints of language? Let the excitement of the experience you are recalling outrun your capacity to catch it by means of speech.

5. Write a paraphrase of the passage, using your own words to capture the imagery of the passage. In your paraphrase, try to recreate the experience as you imagine it. Write it as if it had happened to you.

CHAPTER 3

THE FIRST R: READING YOUR TEXT

Reading well, no matter what the context, calls for you to step into some language system and look at the world from its perspective.

PAUL GRAY AND JAMES VAN OOSTING[1]

The phone message said a group of pastors and laity had called to request a workshop. The topic? "The Oral Reading of Scripture." As a group they wanted to know what they could do to improve their techniques of speaking scripture. Was there some way, they asked, that we could make the public reading of scripture more lively and engaging?

I was delighted to learn of their interest in improving the quality of their presentations of scripture. They sensed that listeners are growing increasingly indifferent to readings and sermons that are flatly delivered. Preachers, readers of scripture, and worship leaders are looking for ways to draw listeners into the 'worlds' of biblical and liturgical texts. In order for these texts to address the primary concerns of listeners' lives, they must be presented in ways that engage the *whole* of human experience, including

- the senses
- the rich resources of individual and collective memory
- the imagination
- human emotion
- human intellect

This is the subject of this chapter.

THE PUBLIC READING OF SCRIPTURE: A LOST ART?

One writer recently wondered whether "book-centered Christianity [was becoming] an anachronism not really connected with people's modes of apprehending reality."[2] Others are fretting that in an age of rapidly accelerating technological change, the practice of reading itself is becoming a lost art. Lynn Miller puts it this way:

> One technology we fear will be left behind is the act of reading itself, something which for many of us epitomized a rich, and private, and highly individualized activity. As the notions of public spaces change–into cyberspace, into further innovations of mass media and mass culture–the fear of losing the private, idiosyncratic world of literature increases also.[3]

If you go into a bookstore on a Friday night, however, you might think that the practice of silent reading is as popular as it has ever been! Readers lounge in comfort with a cup of coffee nearby, "lost" in literature of all kinds. Public spaces for silent reading are readily available in libraries and bookstores. There does not seem to be much evidence that reading is becoming a lost art, even as electronic technology creates all kinds of public discourse and sites for interaction. Books are highly marketable commodities on the Internet. One popular television talk show host, Oprah Winfrey, even conducts book discussions on her show. Whether the "new" media encourage or discourage the practice of reading continues to be open for debate.

One thing that we can be certain of is that the new technology is having an impact on the way we speak and listen. Those of us who preach, read scripture, and plan worship experiences these days are only beginning to get our bearings within the vortex of this communications revolution. We are pressed to examine the ways we organize our material for preaching and present printed texts. We do well when we whet a listener's appetite for scriptures and sermons that take seriously the orality of these presentational acts. When Christians gather for public worship, preachers and oral readers of texts have the opportunity to more deeply involve the congregants in an experience of biblical texts by means of the voice and body.

Preachers, in the company of all public readers and rhetors, are still haunted by Plato's attack on the public readers and rhetors of his day. The truth is "out there," said Plato, existing as ideal forms that human beings can only represent imperfectly. Public readers and rhetors are so far removed from the "truth" that they are all style and delivery, with no content to their (so-called) "art." It is simply a waste of one's time to pursue something that has such little substance as the "art" of public reading or speaking.

Every Sunday morning in virtually every congregation that I know of someone stands up before the group and reads scripture aloud. That person or someone else then offers some kind of *oral* interpretation of those texts (in the form of a sermon) and attempts to help listeners understand how the texts offer good news. Those who were calling to ask for a workshop on *how* to do these readings respect the tradition of reading scripture aloud but also were responding to the demands of the communicative context in which we live.

MINING OLD TRADITIONS FOR NEW GOLD

Two traditions of interpreting scripture will help us answer their concern. The first tradition has been identified by various names: "communicative reading," "oral study of literature," "oral interpretation," or simply, "interpretation." At the time that I entered formal graduate study in communication, it provided a better conceptual framework and set of practices for the oral study of scripture than did biblical scholarship. Reading a text aloud to appreciate both its logical and emotive content in order to share the experience of the literature with an audience was once recognized as a valuable form of interpretation.

When it came to reading *biblical* literature, the late Charlotte Lee, one of the primary teachers in the field, assumed that "the Bible, like all other great literature, must be read aloud to realize its full potential."[4] Her voice joined others arising from the field that have, for a long period of time, "magnified" the public reading of scripture "lest the people might not otherwise hear the Bible or might neglect reading it at home."[5] Now, however, these assumptions are being contested within the discipline itself. "Oral interpretation" has taken a turn away from its focus on "literature" and toward the study of performance in culture. *Performance studies* examines and produces a widening range of cultural events, ranging from theatrical performances to street demonstrations, from street corner rap to storytelling, from festivals to personal conversation. The formal study of human performance is no longer constrained by narrow, pejorative associations with theater arts nor is it bound to printed texts. It believes that human beings are fundamentally performing creatures "who engage in an ongoing process of giving speech to their thoughts and feelings."[6] This means that it is through performances of various kinds that we humans construct, constitute, and sustain our cultural and individual identities. Ideas, theories, and interpretive strategies that come from the discipline of performance studies have made an impact on a growing number of disciplines that inform the study of preaching. One set of gains means other emphases are lost. For example, one thing that performance studies has lost is a ready rationale for an oral study of the Bible or any other kind of "traditional literature." In fact, "textual objects" of any sort or "textualism" of any kind are suspected by one influential thinker in the discipline as a "fundamentalism," an inhibiting construct, which "makes it difficult to rethink performance."[7]

Those of us who teach the expressive performance of language and literature in the seminary share the conviction that the subject still has much to teach preachers and lay readers of the Bible not only about technique but also about its meaning as a communicative event.[8] Although it is harder to drop one's hand into this swirling sea of performance theory and retrieve something tangible that offers encouragement for this work, there are now new signs of interest for it in biblical scholarship.

This turn away from literature and toward a study of performance in culture has happened at a time when biblical scholarship has joined with other kinds of communication studies to reassess the orality of scripture. Tom Boomershine is a biblical scholar and storyteller who tells us that "changes in communications systems are related to profound shifts in modes of perception and thought, patterns of cultural formation, and religious values."[9]

New points of common interest between performance studies and biblical studies hold promise for the study of both oral reading of scripture and preaching. What performance studies has gained in the expansion of its research boundaries is a new and revitalized sense of its value to the study of human communication and culture. By pressing us past a preoccupation with literary texts, Dwight Conquergood reasons that "performance-sensitive ways of knowing...will extend (our) understanding of multiple dimensions and offer a wider range of meaningful action."[10] Included within that "wider range of meaningful action" is a performance-sensitive study of oral reading and preaching that will help close the distance, for example, between "literate" and "nonliterate" cultures, and between classical, Eurocentric homiletics and theories of preaching drawn from other cultural histories and experiences. At the same time, biblical scholarship is taking "orality" quite seriously. Texts and traditions of interpreting them lie in the dynamic space between "writing" and "speech."

My hope for this book is to rekindle an interest in oral reading of scripture, the recital of biblical texts, and retelling biblical stories along lines suggested by biblical texts, and thereby to feed the preacher's imagination and performance in preaching. What Robert Frost once said still resonates, especially as a direction for preaching from biblical texts: "Expression in oral reading rather than intelligent comment is made the test of appreciation."[11]

FINDING NEW REASONS FOR THE
ORAL STUDY OF SCRIPTURE

We need to build a new rationale for a study of scripture that is sensitive to its orality and value as a text for performance. We can build this new rationale on three planks. First, *effective oral reading of biblical texts deepens and enhances liturgical communication.* When those pastors and lay leaders were calling to ask if I was willing to offer a workshop in the oral reading of scripture, they were expressing their interest in deepening and enhancing the *experience* and communicative value of corporate worship. They were acknowledging that worship is (among other things) a series of speech acts. Charles Bartow writes: "Worship is an experience in which we listen to and talk with God and one another."[12] Christian worship is a communal performance in which we enact through speech and gesture our identities as Christians and demonstrate to others and ourselves our collective beliefs about God and what God has done in Jesus Christ.

What we as Christians seek in worship is an encounter with God through communion with Christ. Our understanding about the nature of Christ's presence among us is undergoing transformation. We are aware of some attempts to relocate Jesus in a history *behind* literary texts. The search for a "historical" Jesus who is the "real" one is getting a lot of attention. Literary texts do not say everything that can be said about what God has done and is doing through the resurrection of Christ. Yet in the performance of liturgy we enact the kinds of texts that can bring us into the mystery of Christ's presence. Worship is, therefore, more than rational assent to ideas and propositions; "the revelation of Jesus' communication does not consist of an intellectual idea; it discloses a way of being."[13]

I remember hearing about a student who had recently graduated from the seminary and taken his first pastorate. I was invited as a guest speaker to the student's congregation, and after the sermon I was standing with my host greeting those who had worshiped with us that day. Several people commented to me how much they appreciated their new pastor's ministry. They pointed out that when he read scripture aloud, it came alive for them.

I asked him about this later. "What do you do with the scripture in worship?" He replied: "Here is one thing to tell your students. Tell them not to simply read it at the beginning of the week and not look at again until the moment before they preach. Tell them to keep coming back to it and ask, 'How should this sound?' then read it aloud several times. It really helps it come alive in you!" Apparently this pastor was discovering that when the scripture becomes alive as a form of human utterance to the reader, it has a better chance of becoming alive in the experience of the listeners.

The public reading of scripture is a speech act that worship leaders can do that makes the presence of Christ "come alive" in the community's hearing. It is one of the formal ways that we "talk" with one another about God and a means by which God "talks" with us. What is at issue is the *quality* of this kind of "talk." Tom Driver characterizes modes of ritual speaking and acting in our churches and culture as "impoverished."[14] This concern is what lies underneath the effort to enliven the public reading of scripture in worship—it is to make the act itself more viable as oral communication.

Reading scripture aloud is an act framed within liturgical performance and is subject to the "rules" of that performance. Rules and conventions for effective performances of scripture vary from one community to another. For example, in some communities of faith, the expectation is that a reader of scripture will not establish eye contact during the reading, lest that action distract the listener from the hearing of the Word. The actual biblical text is displayed as a sacred object by being carried in a procession, then placed upon a lectern or stand. The text itself may be richly ornamented and put on display, thus endowing its presence in the community as a prominent "voice."

In other communities the participants are expected to carry their own personal Bibles into worship and "follow along" in silence while the preacher or reader reads the text aloud and then offers interpretative comments on it. They may even be asked to read aloud and in unison from Bibles distributed in the seats or to read antiphonally in one of varied forms of responsive readings. Electronic technology has now made it possible to project texts on screens, making books or other printed matter unnecessary.

Some communities perform texts together through congregational singing or chanting.

The practices of reading the Bible in worship are as varied as the traditions of liturgical performance in which they arise and will continue to take new expressive forms as electronic technology shapes corporate worship practices. Yet even on that vast, shifting landscape, there will certainly be a place for one who will stand and orally present the words of scripture as printed in the Bible. I do not foresee electronic technology eclipsing the importance of this traditional means of addressing the community with words from a sacred book.

In fact, given the burgeoning variety of choices for "reading" scripture in corporate worship, I see an opportunity for this traditional means of speaking the scriptures to take on renewed importance as a "special" communicative event within the performance of the liturgy. What was once routinized in worship may become evocative in this new climate of liturgical expression.

Not long ago, I attended a worship service in a Benedictine monastery near my home. The service is open to the community and is held in an old barn on the property, refurbished for use as a worship center. There was standing room only in the space, and the experience itself was so richly textured that I can scarcely devote the space here to give it a full descriptive report. But I will say that I was quite taken with the way the scriptures were orally performed.

Two lay readers in that community had emerged with a special vocation for leading this part of worship. Neither of these two readers was particularly trained as an actor or an oral interpreter. They did, however, grasp the idea that such an act of leadership in worship required certain competencies—an understanding of worship, prayerful attention, and study of what the text was saying, how the priest would use the text in the homily, and what vocal and physical behaviors would evoke an affective response to the texts when read aloud. I heard many people compliment them after the service by saying, "I had never *heard* it that way before!"

In what other place in our lives do we bear witness to one who stands in front of the gathering and reads aloud to us from a book? Like the soloist in the choir, the reader of scripture may become one of a growing ensemble of liturgical performers who command our respect and attention as the bearer of words from a sacred text.

READING DRAMATIZES THEOLOGY

The second plank in our rationale is this: *effective oral reading of biblical texts is embodied theology.* In the request to me from those pastors and lay leaders was not only a concern for enriching liturgical communication but also the echo of some theological convictions about the Bible. In their request was an affirmation of the Bible's importance as an authoritative guide for Christian faith and practice. We read the Bible aloud because we still believe that it is crucial to our understanding of a Judeo-Christian ethic of justice and liberation; the Bible remains a locus for God's revelation to Israel, the church, and the world of human affairs.

Leander Keck suggests, however, that confidence in the Bible's capacity to speak a word from God has dangerously eroded in many communities. "Today, talk of God's Word through fallible forms has been replaced by concern to identify the ideological character of the biblical texts as a whole."[15] The Bible is held in such scrutiny that we keep it at a "safe" distance, limiting its capacity to speak, to question, to interrogate, to comfort, or to confront. Poor, indifferent public readings muffle it further, aggravate confusion over what texts mean, and deaden the Bible's presence and vitality even in the communities for which it was written.

Another concern arises from parts of the Bible that are experienced by some as "texts of terror." Mary Catherine Hilkert warns that "the conviction that the Christian assembly gathers to be shaped by the text can be dangerous" to women, Jews, gays and lesbians, or "whoever functions as the subordinated, rejected, or demonized 'other'."[16] Ron Allen feels that sometimes it is necessary to preach *against* such texts in order to proclaim God's *good* news.[17] Ellen Davis acknowledges that the writers of both testaments were not "at all times successful in upholding the mystery and radical grace of God's presence," but warns against writing off texts with an attitude of "moral superiority."[18] Keck wants to make the Bible a "companion" more than a "useful object"; he wants to allow its "mythological character to restore our imagination" rather than start fights over "what it means." To do so, we must find ways to "develop a new relation to the Bible, and to begin afresh to think everything through."[19]

To make the effort to enliven the public reading of scripture is to work in collaboration with God's spirit to make the Bible a "companion" by creating a deeper and more enhanced experience of worship. It means that we bring the resources of our God-given imaginations—our thoughts, our experiences, our convictions and questions—to the task of speaking scripture. It also means that we bring our voices and physical presence into the act to enable a biblical text to "speak" within the growing cacophony of voices that address us. The primary responsibility an oral reader has is to "enable the hearers to enter the world that Scripture discloses and thus make a genuine choice about whether they will live there."[20]

To consider this kind of effort often awakens resistances of all kinds that also have theological implications. There is, for example, a lingering assumption in consciousness and in memory that since the Bible is "sacred," its content will be sufficiently communicated when read aloud, regardless of how skillful or inept, how prepared or unprepared the reader is. Since anybody who can read can also read aloud, a reader need not make a special effort because the words can "speak" for themselves.

There are other times when resistances to this effort are organized around the word *dramatic*. I have often heard the objection: "I don't want to become too 'dramatic'!" I take this to mean that the reader does not want to call attention to his or her gifts (or lack thereof) for animated speech and gesticulation that have little or nothing to do with what is being read. It recalls a period in the history of speech instruction when the content and meaning of literary materials were subsumed to the vocal artistry and histrionics of "elocutionists."[21]

Elocution was a thorough and extensive training program within speech education. It involved exercising the speaker's voice and body so that the speaker might "give proper expression to the best thought" offered either by "great authors" or by the speaker.[22] The challenge to any speaker at that time was to make oneself understood in large auditoriums. Voices that were audible, flexible, and full of variety in pitch, tone, and attitude were requirements for public speaking and reading of texts before there were microphones. Developing one's vocal and physical dexterity to meet the demands of communicating speeches and texts was considered a means to an end, not ends in themselves. Effective public reading, like any other form of public address, meant achieving a balance of emphasis between the speaker, what the speaker was saying, and whom the speaker was addressing. Elocutionists placed primary emphasis on the skill and technique of the speakers in reading scripture aloud.

Yet we can also see how the pendulum swung away from such concerns. We may laugh at the elocutionists' posturing in the dimming recesses of our memory, but we have paid a high price for neglecting this kind of study. Most of us attended seminaries where the study of scripture was conducted with virtually no regard for training public readers of scripture. With the remarkable exception of Princeton Theological Seminary, relatively few schools offer courses in which theological students perform and practice an oral study of biblical texts. The neglect is nothing new. S. S. Curry complained nearly a century ago that "there is no well-defined conception or realization of the power of the living voice to interpret [a biblical text's] meaning."[23] Now the study of scripture is conducted almost completely in silence. There is very little sense of the value of "sounding" scriptures in order to study them, much less some determination of *how* we should speak them aloud in corporate worship. Perhaps the old departed elocutionists were so excessive in their emphasis on mannerisms and gesticulations that they scared us off from oral studies and renderings of scripture. However, we are seeing the consequences of silent, detached, and solitary readings of biblical texts. Public readers are ill-prepared for the demands of reading aloud, and listeners are indifferent to the content and claims of Bible texts and overly dependent on "professionals" to explain what the scriptures mean.

Now the pendulum has swung again, this time in the direction of scripture's audience and readership. Some forms of criticism emphasize that the reader is the sole creator of meaning. Authors are "fictions," the meanings of texts indeterminate outside the reader's subjectivity, and the act of interpretation itself extremely politicized. Interpretation is an act that privileges some readings while silencing others.

We live in a highly politicized climate for interpretation. All interpretations are contested. Why should we be surprised at anyone's lack of confidence in his or her choice for interpretation–oral, dramatic, or otherwise? Still, one of the ghosts that haunts and inhibits the work of the oral, public reader of scripture is that of the platform performer of long ago whose excessive concentration on vocal technique and style puts us off. That image of performance dominates the electronic media today. One woman said to me in a class, "I don't want to be too dramatic in my reading because I want to maintain the theological integrity of the text." *Dramatic* lives in our consciousness as a pejorative term that often drives a wedge between what we want to speak (a text or message) and the way we want to say it. This perception inhibits the desire to improve one's public reading of a biblical text. One feels that to improve one's public reading is to intrude on the way that God is addressing the hearer through the text. There are other ways we can use *dramatic* as a term that integrates our theological and stylistic interests where public reading is concerned.

Being dramatic is nothing more than responding to a basic human impulse to show and tell. Showing and telling are actions "based in conflict and dramatic in nature."[24] Something in our characters as human beings urges us to tell our stories to one another as a way of showing how conflicts achieved (or failed to achieve) resolution. In the telling, we "show" ourselves on the various "stages" we inhabit and reveal ourselves to be competent performers of the narratives we make.

What flows from showing and telling are two kinds of traditions. On the one hand, "tellings" can evolve into oral and literary narrative traditions; "showings" can develop into either ritual or theatrical traditions. All showings and tellings are communicative acts because they presuppose that there will be a response from those who receive them. In fact, audiences are also "actors," because they collaborate with speakers in making the message event meaningful.

When a reader stands in the assembly to orally present the scripture, that reader is standing at a place where showing and telling converge. By reading the text aloud, he or she is "reoralizing" the written tradition of scripture; the performed text is a gateway by which reader and listener enter into the experience of an "other" who also struggles with God's presence in human experience. It is through this sort of encounter that we achieve a richer, fuller understanding of our own situations.

By standing (as the reader will most likely do) in the assembly of worshipers, the reader is taking a particular part in the performance of a sacred ritual. The reader shows that he or she is visible and radically present in the performance as a willing participant. The reader also shows through the public reading that the scriptures are a highly valued and privileged voice and presence in the ritual, a voice that will evoke responses from all who listen. The reader is the one who mediates the voice and presence of the scriptures by lending his or her own voice and presence and allowing the scripture to "speak." He or she "draws on both oral and written traditions" to speak in a manner that is "more oral-centered than print-centered."[25]

A public reading is an embodied mediation that involves what the text says, how the reader speaks it, how the listener hears it, and what God might say through it. Mediation might be imagined as a web of encounters. The one who will read the text in public encounters the words of the text by reading it in silence, then aloud. As the reader studies the text by asking questions of it, by investigating its historical and literary context, by deciding what the author of the text seems to be saying to its auditors and where to place vocal emphasis, the reader opens him- or herself up to an encounter with God's word through the text. It is the experience of that encounter that the reader intends to share in the act of reading that text to a group of listeners. To convey meaning, the reader uses the resources of her or his voice, body, thought, and attitude. This is what makes it "embodied." It is an act of mediation that communicates the thought, attitude, and spirit of the biblical text to its auditors. This dynamic of "words becoming flesh" is what makes a reading dramatic.

Dramatic is a viable term that describes how the text functions as effective and incarnational communication. Dramatic reading is not so named because it employs stylistic conventions appropriate to the theater. It is dramatic because it effects a transaction between the biblical text and its several auditors. In this transaction, the words printed on the page become an experience in literature, liturgy, and theology for readers and hearers. What the preacher (or some other public reader) aims for is not simply the oral transmission to the congregation of the words that appear on the page but a lively encounter through which a text (that which is written and read from a page) becomes a form of aesthetic communication (a creative act in time in which meanings are made).

This is another place where *performance* is a helpful word–it clarifies our theology of communication for speaking texts aloud. Performance is usually used as a way of describing the work of the individual in reading scripture aloud. The word literally means "form coming through" and can describe the dynamics of oral reading. From this angle, we see one who is preparing to read scripture to the assembly. He or she has worked on understanding the text itself, how it is constructed, and what it is trying to say to any who would hear it. The performer also works at placing the resources of her body and voice into the service of what the text might be saying or doing in the assembly. The mediation of the text's multiple meanings takes concrete shape in the public reading. A text's form and structure are transformed into a living presence forged by the mediation between text, reader, and hearer. Present in the performance event are these participants:

1. the reader, displaying and enacting herself as bearer of a sacred text;
2. an author or maker of a text, implied by the text but "bodied forth" in the reading;
3. the audience, animated as collaborators in making the reading meaningful and engaging;
4. the many voices of Christ's spirit, addressing the assembly through the liturgical act of reading. Performance is a term that helps us catch and hold the meaning of this emergent moment in liturgical time.

Yet performance has wider theological implications and applications. Nicholas Lash uses the term to create an image of the Christian congregation's relationship to biblical texts. "The fundamental form of the Christian interpretation of scripture," says Lash, "is the performance of the biblical text."[26] Here Lash means that we are to construe "the life, activity and organization of the believing community" as a "'rendering', bearing witness to, one whose words and deeds, discourse and suffering, 'rendered' the truth of God in human history."[27] So we can say with Lash that the form of the scripture "comes through" in the life of the congregation.

Performance describes the work of the public reader who offers an oral, incarnational, and communicative act as an interpretation of scripture in the gathered assembly. It also describes the vital relationship that a Christian community has with those written texts it has deemed "sacred" and capable of having revelatory power. What they reveal and disclose is the story of Jesus as a story of God's work in the world. Performance indicates those practices that a community does in the name of Christ and that are empowered, interrogated, inspired, and even judged by Christ's risen presence.

READING AS SACRED PLAY

Now we lay the third plank: *Reading the Bible aloud is playful.* When the reader settles into that comfortable chair in the old, used bookstore on a rainy Saturday afternoon, it is a pleasurable event. Reading is one of the many ways that we human beings "play." It is a form of "free activity, standing quite consciously outside 'ordinary life' as being 'not serious'" but at the same time utterly and completely absorbing.[28] Freedom to play with language in this and many other ways is what makes us human.

I want to emphasize this image of reading as play because I believe that a spirit of play is sorely needed for reading the Bible in public. We all shudder when we think of those pieces we had to memorize at church or school, our standing and stiffly declaiming what we learned from a page. Or we squirm when we think of the awkward, obligatory fumbling with a text we are likely to hear on Sunday morning. What we are after is a means of releasing the words from a text into a lively and expressive form of speech; we aim to transform the record of an experience into an experience itself. To read aloud and to read well is an invitation to play, that is, to willingly participate in the conversation between a biblical text, its authorship, and the many different audiences that it draws. It is "an experience involving not simply the isolation of themes or extraction of ideas but also the engagement of the senses and the play of writer and reader, of competing voices, and of timing and rhythm."[29]

There is no such thing as "pure" play; play is governed by some kind of "rules." Reading the Bible aloud is a form of play that is subject to some rules. You and I might disagree about what those rules should be. In what ways shall I demonstrate my respect for scripture when I read in public? What choices shall I make? Am I to place myself strictly at the service of the words on the page to the extent that I do not make eye contact? In what ways is my reading artful? Is a public reading of scripture more like conversation, acting, or public speaking? Am I free to memorize a text and speak the words "as if" they are my own? Or am I getting too far away from the "holy" Bible when I do this? Questions such as these are the subject of the next chapter. Right now I want to mention one rule that I believe governs our public reading of biblical texts. It is certainly a contested rule, because it has to do with the web of relationships between the reader of a text, its author, and its audience. I believe that the primary task of the public reader of scripture is to "reproduce the self created by the writer in the text for an audience."[30]

Interpreters of written texts are reaching widely different conclusions about the "presence" of authors. They differ greatly in their answers to the following set of questions:

- Is there such a thing as *an* "author"? Or is the question of *authorship* more complex?
- In what ways is a "literary self" presented in a written work?
- Who, for example, is writing the gospels?
- Who wrote the epistles attributed to Paul?
- There is a coherent, recognizable persona, a "self" of some kind that is named "John" that writes the Fourth Gospel. What is the relationship between the "linguistic" self that is presented in the Gospel and the "historical" self that we identify as "John"?
- How important is that relationship?

Assumptions vary widely as to the distance between the literary and historical selves of authors of texts.

On one end of the spectrum are those who hold that clues to the meaning of texts lie strictly within an author's intent. The one who is writing a text is the ultimate source of meaning. If we could only adequately identify that writer's circumstances for composition and discern the theological motives, we would have the key to a text. A variation of this position is that God is the ultimate author of any and all biblical texts. Writers of biblical text are merely inspired vehicles or human instruments whom God uses to get things written down. To adequately interpret a biblical text then means to apprehend what God is saying to all readers, regardless of their social and temporal locations.

On the other end are those who say that the author is a "fiction," that is, that the "I" who is writing is simply a construct for holding together the writing itself. What gives meaning to that text is not an author, but the one who is reading. What replaces "God" as the "ultimate" author at this end of the spectrum is a set of culturally bound rules and conventions for writing and producing texts. Readers and interpreters create meaning out of clues, traces, and impressions present as "texts."

I believe that one who is reading a biblical text in and for corporate worship, and certainly one who is reading a biblical text in preparation to preach, assumes the presence, not absence, of biblical authors. In doing so, a reader assumes something about the presence of God in the composition and development of biblical texts. The language on the page is coming from somewhere, from some place in time, in the play of shadow and light deriving from some part of God's revelation of God's Self to human beings in particular times and places. Texts are presentations of voices and selves, and they call for an infinite array of embodiments, enactments, and interpretations from readers and their communities. Interpretations and commitments arising from them are performed both in worship and in the events of everyday life that is lived in light of Christian faith. These texts have power because they are resonances of events in God's self-disclosure. They require us to tune our ears, eyes, senses, and intelligence for what God's spirit might be saying to us now through these echoes of other times and places. No printed text, biblical or otherwise, can simply speak for itself. It requires collaboration from those it addresses to "make sense."

The communicative power of biblical texts to speak in the assembly is limited. In order to "speak" more fully and completely, they must become literally part of our bodies. We read them with our eyes and have oral/aural memories of them being spoken, interpreted, preached, and sung. Words and phrases, narrative and poetic structures of thought interweave with episodes, images, anecdotes, and emotional memories retained in our own experience. The meanings of biblical texts are certainly not self-evident. As they come to us, they are fixed on pages, silent and mass produced in a bewildering variety of translations and expressions in a widening array of media. The purpose of reading aloud is to give voice, bodily shape, and expression to the "presences" we find evoked by biblical texts.

Reading a biblical text aloud is an intentional act of turning something as fixed and abstract as a text into concrete, embodied human speech. It is a convergence of language and action, of "saying" and "doing." What is "present" at this site of convergence is a "realness," a "substantiation," and an embodiment of "otherness." This "otherness" can be known through transcendence and disclosure. George Steiner declares that human speaking that is alive with focus, motive, and intentionality has this quality of "realness." Any *coherent* understanding of what language is and does, of how language performs, of the capacity of human speech to communicate meaning and feeling is, in the final analysis, underwritten by an assumption of God's presence.[31] It is this presence that prompts the act of reading aloud and, in collaboration with the ones reading and listening, comes through the reading as the sound and shape of human speech and gesture. It is through such oral, embodied interpretive acts that we "reorder our existences and the universe in which we exist."[32]

THE SIGNIFICANCE OF PUBLIC READING

I build a liturgical, theological, and playful rationale for reading texts aloud because I want to do three things: First, I want to open a window in the preacher's homiletical imagination. I believe that to engage in an oral/aural study of scripture is to open oneself to new questions, interrogations, inspirations, and possibilities for presentation. It is, as Leander Keck hopes, a way to help the scriptures become more of a companion in our daily lives, while anticipating it will have a fuller voice and presence in worship.

Second, I believe that this kind of commitment to scripture will heighten the communicative power and the aesthetic value of the liturgical climate in which we preach. A reading of a text that "bodies forth" is a text that "calls to" a listener in an explicit way. It gives a text a communal dimension that a solitary and silent reading does not. I would much rather preach in an environment where a reading or some other form of expressive presentation of a sacred text has caused listeners to care about what I might have to say in regard to that text.

Finally, I want to find ways to instigate the reading of the Bible in a culture that either fights about it, fights *with* it, or ignores it altogether. "Reading" and "biblical study" have become the province of professional interpreters who, until only recently, conducted their critical study in the silence of the study. The command of critical apparatus and traditions of interpretation and/or appeals to one's ecclesial authority tend to take the Bible out of the hands, hearts, and imaginations of those to whom we speak. Taking the Bible seriously as a work of theological imagination, as residue of active oral and ritual practice that begets new forms of expressive communication, and as "play" in God's drama of self-disclosure will certainly empower new "readers" and new reasons for preaching.

The motive and substance of this work is not easily explained as an "academic discipline of inquiry" with clearly defined boundaries. One approaches the prospect of corporate worship with hunger, desire for experience, love, devotion, and even perhaps a measure of fear and suspicion. We bring the raw materials of our experience and hopes for meaningful transactions between divine and human "word." When we are in the presence of God in worship and participating in the ensemble performance of praise, the boundaries that divide human knowledge and expertise are quickly blurred.

Workshop 3: Public Reading as a Communicative Art

In this workshop, we will assume that the public reading of a text in worship can be a form of aesthetic communication. The reader understands that his or her task is to help the listener recreate the *experience* available in the text on the stage of the listener's imagination.

A text from the Bible may be understood as a work of narrative, lyrical, or rhetorical art. It is a creation of someone's imagination and conforms to certain aesthetic principles in composition. What the biblical writer is attempting to do is share an experience of revealed truth through available literary forms. What prompts the experience available in the text is an encounter with God, and it is made meaningful, coherent, and understandable through the writer's encounter with available traditions of revelation and interpretation.

The reader enters into the world presented by the text—its arrangement of myths and symbols, its own universe of meaning, the effect of its linguistic structure and content—in order to engage the writer's interpretation of revelation. In order to understand that experience and open it up for the audience, the reader must find points of contact with the text, that is, those parts of the reader's own experience that are illuminated by the text.

The relationship the reader will establish with the text is itself complex. Because the text comes from a perspective totally "other" than the reader's own, parts of the writer's experience must remain in the realm of mystery. At some points the text will interrogate the reader, and at other points the reader will interrogate the text! If we are honest with one another and ourselves, we will also admit that sometimes we actually see ourselves *in* the text, hear ourselves being addressed and implicated by it. Leander Keck suggests that this is what "living with" the Bible looks like. He says "it is only by living with it that we can be influenced by it and can appropriate its ways of thinking and its vocabulary so that we know ourselves as part of the same family."[33] It is this experience of living with the biblical text that the reader wants to share with a group of listeners.

To understand that act of sharing as *art* means the act is conforming to established aesthetic principles for the oral interpretation of literature. Like the actor, the public reader aims to evoke an empathic response from the listener by making the situation presented by the text as vivid and compelling as possible. The reader wants to close the distance between the listener's own situation and that presented by the interpreted work. I had a teacher of play directing who instructed us to "make him care" about the characters in the play.

What if we were in this same situation? How would we feel? If I were a woman who had been suffering from internal bleeding for twelve years (see Mark 5), how would I feel if there was hope for a cure? We might ask with whom the writer wants us to identify in the passage. Where do the writer's sympathies seem to be? Our task as readers is to guide the listener into the situation presented by the text by attending to the human predicament we find expressed there by the various "speakers" in the text.

To effect this kind of identification between the text and the audience, we use a different set of conventions than does the secular actor. An actor creates empathy with a character through the arts of impersonation. The actor creates his or her impression of a character by assuming the character's mannerisms, by affecting vocal and physical behaviors and a manner of dress appropriate to that character, and by speaking as if he or she *were* that character. The text for this kind of performance is internalized by the actor and is written as a script or a monologue.

The performer of the *biblical* text, however, maintains the words, structure, and unity of the text *as it appears in scripture.* The performer may or may not choose to internalize the text, but, in any case, works to speak "as if" the words of the text were the performer's own. The reader as performer of the text does not attempt to impersonate the narrator or any of the others who "speak" in the text. He or she does not "represent" a speaker through impersonation, but "presents" him or her as a kind of "conductor, who orchestrates the text through suggestive vocal and physical action."[34]

This approach to reading is like that of the "communicative act" model in that it is concerned with clearly and coherently conveying the writer's meaning to an audience by means of reading aloud. Its primary goal is the thought and motivation of the author in the transaction. In this model, the reader is effective when he or she successfully evokes empathy between the predicament presented in a text and the situation of the listener. The performance is a sharing of the experience that the performer has had with the text, vocally, physically, and emotionally expressing the *effect* the text has had, and closing the aesthetic distance that exists between the world of the text, the reader, and the listener.

FOR PRACTICE

1. Read the text aloud. (For our purposes here, I suggest the story of the Syrophoenician woman in Mark 7).
2. Identify the "speakers" in the text. Also identify who is "present" but is *not* speaking in this particular text. What is the situation of each of these? What do they *want* more than anything else? Where are the sources of conflict between the speakers themselves? What are the obstacles that keep the speaker from getting what he or she wants?
3. Read the text aloud and focus your attention on one speaker or the other. Place yourself in that speaker's predicament and, using the words given in the text, read the speaker's words "as if" they were your own. What emotional range is there?
4. Now read the text from the perspective of another speaker. Emphasize his or her words. Did you read the speaker's words as actions or reactions to something or someone else?
5. Now read the text and "orchestrate" the situation by suggesting the attitudes of the different speakers in relationship to one another.
6. Practice speaking this text as if you were an eyewitness to it. One way to increase the sense of immediacy of the eyewitness account is to internalize the words of the text, that is, to speak the words "as if" they were your own without the text in front of you. If you do feel the need to use the text in your performance, do not make any attempt to hide or disguise that fact. Go ahead and incorporate the text into your performance, but as a memory aide. Think of how a choir member holds the score through the performance. The score

helps to *enable* the singer's performance, but throughout, the listener can tell that it is the score that is serving the performer, not the performer awkwardly constrained by the score.

CHAPTER 4

THE SECOND R: THE RECITATION OF SCRIPTURE

In telling and listening to the stories of Jesus, early Christians made connections with their own lives that made clear to them how God was present.

THOMAS E. BOOMERSHINE[1]

The members of the Bible study group were angry with the interim pastor. They had been meeting together for quite some time with the minister, who had just left for another church. In those weekly meetings they would study the lectionary texts together, and then some of them would agree to serve as readers and liturgists. Still others would agree to commit upcoming gospel lessons to memory in order to recite them in worship. Now the interim pastor wanted to "take back" the gospel lesson and was reading those lessons himself in a flat and unengaging style. The members of the group, *especially those who enjoyed reciting the gospel lessons,* felt as if something important to their worship was missing.

What happened? *The previous minister had come to value the importance of an oral study of biblical texts, not only for performance in worship, but for his own interpretation of those texts for preaching.* Every week in the study group the minister would listen to the texts read aloud and discussed over and over again. Then, over time, some of the members of the group developed the discipline of speaking the texts from memory. The minister himself did not think he was particularly gifted in this regard, any more than he felt gifted in singing. He was, however, grateful for the opportunity to hear these texts spoken aloud because they deepened his understanding of what was being said by placing him in the 'story world' of the gospels; in other words, the oral arts of reading and recitation awakened his imagination for preaching. The purpose of this chapter is to introduce the preacher to the benefits of oral recitation of scripture—for listening, for study, and for speaking.

RECLAIMING THE VALUE OF RECITATION FOR UNDERSTANDING SCRIPTURE

A few years ago I was invited to participate in a group recitation of the entire gospel of Mark. The international Network of Biblical Storytellers was planning the performance. "NOBS," based in Dayton, Ohio, understands itself as "an international organization whose mission is to communicate the sacred stories of the biblical tradition."[2] Every year this organization sponsors a "Gathering" at a different site, where new techniques for the oral performance of biblical texts are learned and practiced. Those who attend the event usually get the chance to listen to a recitation of an entire book of the Bible, or at least a collection of extended narratives. In workshops they learn to "internalize" the structure, words, and images of selected biblical texts and study them for both content and emphasis in order to learn to speak the words of the texts from memory; that is, to speak the words as if the words of the text were the speaker's own. The aim for this work is to heighten a sense of "the presence of personal witnesses"[3] by converting a form of literate communication into speech and enactment.

NOBS is but one of a number of groups that have surfaced in recent years that experiment with the oral presentation of biblical material. Their experiments are guided by the conviction that biblical material as it exists in print came into being as a result of a rich and complex interanimation of oral and literate modes of communication. This material can be studied orally as texts for speaking and performance. According to Walter Ong, texts are "arrested utterances." Writing "only interrupts the utterance as discourse, for the text is not truly a text until it is read, which is to say, until it is reintroduced into discourse."[4]

NOBS sponsors performance of texts in a manner that respects their printed form but also responds to the demands of oral communication.[5] It imagines that the printed text serves as a kind of script for the speaker's own performance of it. The speaker selects language for utterance that is quite close to the language of the text, then employs vocal and physical behaviors for the performance that are suggested by its thought and emotional qualities.[6]

Reciting the text at an event such as an NOBS Gathering does not mean slavish adherence to the words as they appear on the page. The performance that results from that kind of preparation would simply be the wooden, oral re-creation of printed words. Preparation for the recitation means learning to speak "by heart" in a way that places the reciter in the role of one who is narrating an event in sacred history. David Rhoads, who regularly performs the text of the gospel of Mark as a solo piece, says that the reciter of a biblical text "reenacts the world of the story in the space on the stage."[7] It is a deliberate and playful blurring of styles, genres, and modes of public address; at different moments in the performance a spoken text is akin to drama, storytelling, or even heightened conversation.

RECITATION AS EVENT

The concept for the performance of the gospel of Mark was this: The entire text of the gospel would be presented in one session of about two hours with an intermission. Each performer was assigned the task of learning one chapter to present in the order set down in the gospel, demonstrating the techniques for reading and recitation that participants learn in the workshops. The chapters would be presented as solo pieces in which the performer would speak as the narrator, adhere closely to the printed words, and "stage" the performance in appropriate ways. The performance would be framed as a worship experience and would begin and end with prayers and praise.

Those of us who were performing hoped that the listeners' relationship to the text of Mark's gospel would be transformed by this experience. Most reading and study of such a text is conducted in silence, except for the occasional reading of a portion of it in worship or Bible study. We hear texts sung occasionally, but it is rare in our faith communities to hear passages recited at all, much less to hear an entire book or even a long biblical narrative. By transforming the entire text of the gospel of Mark into a form of speech, we wanted the listeners to appreciate the value of that text not only as a "book" but also as oral communication.

THE MEANING OF RECITATION

An oral/aural experience of biblical texts urges a different sort of participation in the life of the text than does a silent reading. For one thing, the *sound* of the text awakens the senses in ways that are different from reading the text in solitary silence. The eye is not the only "window to the soul." To hear a text means to see the world of the text unfold in the mind's eye. Characters and settings written into biblical texts come to life in the listener's imagination, arousing a listener's empathy for a character's situation and collapsing the distance separating the world of the listener from the world of the text. Empathy makes identification with the characters in their situations more possible.

In a recitation or in a public reading, the sounding of a text makes the event *public,* that is, those in attendance become aware of their roles and responsibilities as "audience." The arts of listening, interpretation, and participation become communal in ways that solitary, silent reading does not permit. Recitation transforms what is found on the space of a page into something heard within a community of listeners. The reciter becomes responsible for leading the listener through the experience that a text recalls so that the experience may resonate in the listener's world of perception.

The reciter of a biblical text has a different kind of relationship to the printed word than does the oral reader. In a public reading, the presence of the text as a revered object is highlighted. The reader respectfully holds it before him- or herself or places it on a lectern. It is clear from a public reading that there is both physical and aesthetic distance between the reader and the text. The bodily presence of the reader is distinct from "the book." In other words, the text for the reading is clearly outside the body of the reader. A reader is the explicit mediating agent between the authorial presence and the listener. The text is understood by both reader and listener to be the "voice" that is initiating the communicative act, a voice that the reader serves by lending his or her voice, body, and degree of understanding to the authorial presence. The reader conveys the impression that he or she has been and is now being addressed by the text. In the public act of reading, a solo reader communicates both the intellectual understanding of the text and the *effect* that text has had on the reader. Some of the perceptions of how to understand that act of reading and the skills required in preparation for it are outlined in the preceding chapter.

In a recitation, the performer of the text collapses the distance between the words of the text and the one who is speaking them. The text is "internalized"; that is, the reciter adopts the author's words and structures of thought in order to address the listener. This allows the reader/reciter to be more physically invested in the transaction by means of fuller eye contact and expressive use of the body. An effective recitation conveys the impression of immediacy that these words are for *this* moment and for *this* occasion, even though they come from another time, place, and occasion. The boundary between performer and author is blurred in this kind of performance.

Although the reciter need not fully impersonate the author through the use of costumes or makeup, he or she does *suggest* authorial presence through the medium of his or her own voice, body language, and personality. Each reciter brings to the performance a sense of self and how that text has affected his or her experience and understanding, in order to embody the authorial presence. At the same time, the reciter maintains aesthetic distance from the "self" that is identified in the text as authorial presence. The listener knows that the one who is reciting is not the same as the one who created the text in the first place, but is intrigued by the fact that he or she is being addressed by that author's words. The reciter does not attempt to *become* the author, only to render the world that the author has recreated using the language of a text and its structures of thought.

RECITATION AS A METHOD OF STUDY:
A PERSONAL EXPERIENCE

The chapter I agreed to perform was the first chapter of the gospel of Mark. The first task for the reciter is to prepare the printed version of the text into an "oral friendly" form. You open any Bible and you see that the text is organized for private, silent reading. Numbers mark chapters and verses, and occasionally the text is also broken up into paragraphs with headings boldly marked. This format contributes to the sense that the gospel is a fragmented series of episodes, teachings, and other forms of address. Although such a format is fine for reading in increments, a sense of the unity of the text is lost.

I found it to be quite difficult to try to learn the text for recitation as long as it sat this way on the page. Tom Boomershine offers a different way of looking at the text and preparing it for recitation. Biblical narratives may be "translated" into "episodes"– memory units of three or four lines of text in which the author briefly describes a setting, introduces a character, gives an account of an event, or makes a transition between events. Boomershine suggests that you can identify "verbal threads,"[8] words and phrases that are repeated throughout the story. Verbal threads may not only help hold the narrative together in one's memory but also give a clue to what points of the narrative the author wants to emphasize. If you take a narrative text and organize it in this way for recitation, you are less intimidated by the prospect of learning it by heart.

After preparing the text in this way and then reading it aloud several times, I started work on a *narrative exegesis* of what I would be reciting. A narrative exegesis of a biblical text attempts to come to terms with the form that it is in. Gospels are blurred literary genres; that is, they resemble stories, sermons, conversations, and bits and pieces of oral instruction and illustration. Narrative exegesis takes the literary qualities of the text itself into account, rather than the historical circumstances that gave rise to it. It sees a text such as the gospel of Mark as a finished and complete work that has unity in all its parts. This work is not without aesthetic value. In traditions of biblical criticism a biblical text has at times been devalued as "low" or "vulgar" approximations of literary art and therefore not worthy of study as literature. Narrative exegesis respects the quality of the work as a form of thought uniquely suited to the author's purposes and as the product of a highly skilled and imaginative writer.

It is also interested in how the text works as communication, especially when it is transformed into speech. "All theories of literature," says Mark Allen Powell, "understand the text as a form of communication through which a message is passed from the author to the reader."[9] This aspect of narrative exegesis is of particular interest to the one who is preparing to recite a passage. In recital, a speaker initiates a form of communication that was itself initiated by an author, using the language that the author chose to address his or her audience. The reciter takes on the responsibility of re-presenting (of presenting *again*) the words found on the page in order to deepen their resonance and expand their capacity to address an audience. The reciter is trying to understand the kind of communication that the text represents.

A reciter plays multiple roles in the single communicative act of recitation. First, the reciter is a "stand-in" for the author, representing the reciter's own attempt to grasp traces of authorial presence in the transaction—what was the one who originated this discourse attempting to do, say, or demonstrate to an audience? The reciter is primarily interested in the "author-in-the-work," that is, in coming to terms with what the implied author is doing *with and through* the work itself. What do the work itself and the techniques of expression that one uses suggest about who is writing the work and what he or she is attempting to do? What particular phrases, literary structures, and forms does the author employ? How have they been translated into other languages and versions? The reciter will amplify the impact of this language by incorporating the oral values of pitch, inflection, pause, and phrasing when speaking it and increasing its effect by employing appropriate gestures.

Finally, the reciter represents for listeners the effect that this discourse might have had on its "original" hearers. In order to render the text for an audience of "new" hearers, the reciter must first "read the text as the *implied* reader...to know everything that the text assumes that the (implied) reader knows and to 'forget' everything that the text does not assume the reader knows."[10]

The reciter represents what he or she believes might have been the implied reader/auditor's questions: What kinds of questions would the author's readers/auditors have asked? What kinds would they *not* have asked?

In performance the reciter initiates a communicative transaction that is based in other transactions that a text suggests and incites. The reciter will become in performance one who addresses a group of listeners, using the text found fixed and printed on a page of the Bible. The primary motive for this address is to facilitate entrance into the "story world" that author, text, and its implied auditors/readers inhabit and there find elements of messages that are appropriate for the world of perception the reciter and his or her auditors inhabit. Narrative exegesis provides a framework for reader and reciter to make sense of two kinds of communicative transactions suggested by a selected text, and to formulate links between them:

- A narrative exegesis helps one to understand a text as a web of transaction between an author, text, and reader/auditor.
- A narrative exegesis helps reciters and audiences understand and evaluate the *performance* of a text as a web of transactions between reciter, text-as-speech, and listener.
- A narrative exegesis tries to understand *what* a text is saying by wrestling with *how* it is saying it.
- A reciter is interested in *how* a text works in order to rehearse *how* he or she will speak it.

FROM NARRATIVE EXEGESIS TO ENSEMBLE PERFORMANCE

Since my ensemble's shared task was to present the gospel in its entirety, the narrative exegete's stress on the unity of the gospel was well taken. The story is one of surprise at God's choice to act in the way the gospel describes. Through Jesus, God acts decisively to invade the domain of "Satan" and establish a foothold for God's own realm (Mk. 3:23–27). Jesus is the designated "Son of God" (1:11) who is ordained, authorized, and empowered by God to "proclaim the good news of God" (1:14) and to teach, heal, and cast out demons on his way to create a new community.

The "new teaching" (1:27b) and the way of discipleship that Jesus outlines are at odds with traditional views of righteousness and concerns those whom society has discredited or nearly forgotten. Moreover, Jesus subverts some traditional expectations of the messianic vocation. His way leads to suffering and death, but anticipates vindication by God through resurrection from the dead (8:30–31).

Resurrection suggests a move toward joy and victory, but the gospel still reads like a tragedy. Although Jesus is able by means of God's power to command demonic spirits, illness, and nature, and, in fact, is ultimately resurrected in the way he anticipates, he is not able to instill faith and obedience among his closest followers. Nor is Jesus able to avoid the worst kind of physical suffering and abandonment, even by God.

The account of Jesus' suffering is far more developed in Mark's gospel than is the account of Resurrection. The events are marked by the disciples' abandonment ("All of them deserted him and fled," 14:50) and later, the failure to obey the divine command to speak the good news of his resurrection ("And they said nothing to anyone, for they were afraid," 16:8b). The plot is unified by Mark's presentation of Jesus as the Son of God. Jesus stands at the center of the action, performing miraculous deeds, teaching with force, wisdom, and authority and eliciting both opposition and faith from those he encounters.

Narrative exegesis is interested in the unity of the work itself and in elements such as characters, events, and settings that contribute to that unity. In my case, I needed to take a close look at the piece of text I had been assigned so that in my performance of it I might contribute to the overall effect of the entire gospel in a helpful way. A recital of an entire gospel by an ensemble of speakers is a wondrously diverse display of styles, personalities, and voices. Since we all agreed to work from the same translation (the *New Revised Standard Version Bible*), the performance would at least sound as if it came from the same text. Yet there was still the possibility that the gospel might not hold together with so many people speaking in seriatim. NOBS encouraged each of us to use a narrative framework to analyze our respective texts for performance. Each of us agreed that we would focus on the importance of characters, events, and settings in our analysis in order to lend a higher degree of unity and coherence to our recital.

Mark makes it clear in the very first verse that the subject of his "good news" is the identity of Jesus. The reader/auditor hears that Mark's central character is the "anointed one" (or "Christ") and the "Son of God." This is the how the evangelist wants to portray Jesus throughout the work. Everything that Jesus does is to be attributed to his identity as "Son of God." Already expectations are heightened. What will the "Son of God" do? How will he be received? This was also a clue to me on what words and phrases from the first chapter I should emphasize when I recited them. I wanted to make it clear what Mark's point of view on Jesus was and how Mark understood Jesus' mission. I also wanted to stress throughout my recitation that what followed was actually good news in spite of the way events would transpire. This meant that the attitude for this section should be that of joyful proclamation.

Mark also introduces a set of characters in the first chapter that will play important parts in the drama. The ministry of John the Baptist, for example, is brought into the context of the good news about Jesus. The way that Mark describes John's physical appearance (v. 6) reminds readers/auditors of other prophetic figures that burst on the scene whenever God was up to something. Until Jesus enters, the only two voices besides the evangelist's that we hear speaking are those of the "prophet Isaiah" and John the Baptist. In reciting this part of the chapter, the performer can amplify this connection further. Each voice is one "crying in the wilderness" and should be heard like that. Both speeches are charged with active verbs, modifiers, and vivid imagery: "send," "prepare," "shout," "cry," "preach," and "baptize" are all examples. I also noticed how many times in this part of the chapter a form of the word *baptize* appears. This is an example of a verbal thread that organizes what Mark is saying and how the listener is hearing what is being said. There are a number of other verbal threads. "Preaching" is one, as is "repentance." See if you can identify others.

When Jesus arrives in the story, it is striking how little is said about him. We know only that he is "from Nazareth of Galilee"

(v. 9). It seems as though Mark wants to *show* us who Jesus is by focusing our attention on *what happens* in the plot rather than *tell* us what we should be thinking. Mark quickly advances his narrative. Jesus is there to be baptized, and in a dramatic disclosure that only the reader/auditor, Jesus, and the evangelist are privy to, God speaks directly to Jesus, declaring him to be "my Son, the Beloved" (v. 11).

Here is where the reciter can make a significant contribution to the telling of the story. *How will God sound?* Since the only character in the story who will hear God is Jesus, will God whisper? Or since Mark wants to fully disclose Jesus' identity to the reader/auditor, will the words of God sound like an announcement? The reciter might want to consult the resources of his or her experience. How does God sound when God speaks to you? Loud and clear? Or "in a still small voice"? Does that fit with what you believe Mark is attempting to say with this story? I tried it different ways and concluded that I would speak God's voice loud and clear in order to link what God says and how God says it to the other voices we have heard thus far.

We have come this far, and still Jesus has not spoken. Instead, the story places us with Jesus in "the wilderness" with "wild beasts" where we are "tempted by Satan" (vv. 12–13). This is one of those places throughout the story where the setting becomes an important element. Mark's contemporaries probably would have associated this account with other "wilderness experiences." God used the wilderness wanderings of Israel, for example, to fashion and clarify Israel's faith and what it meant to be in covenant with God. The wilderness is a dangerous place where anything can happen. It is in the wilderness that the Satan character is first introduced. Wilderness is not only a place of wandering and wondering about one's vocation but also a place for warfare. Mark does not linger long here; his account is not nearly so developed as Matthew's and Luke's. It conceals a lot from us and, for me, does not end with a satisfying pronouncement of Jesus' victory over Satan. The "testing" seems to conclude, but this is no rearguard action; the warfare has just begun. The plot will begin to develop as Jesus calls disciples but also encounters opposition. Jesus' invasion of Satan's domain will mean suffering and some losses. We will soon learn that John himself is one of the first casualties and points to what is in store for Jesus. Throughout the story John's fate will point to Jesus' own.

Wilderness is also a potent image in contemporary spirituality. Which of us has not felt that we have been driven, almost against our will, by a "spirit" that certainly is not ours, into some place of spiritual isolation? It is the power of that image, reinforced by our knowledge of wilderness experiences throughout scripture, that gives communicative value to this setting. Mark is taking great pains to put the auditor in the company of Jesus before Jesus even calls his disciples. We are made to be "insiders" by sharing in Jesus' baptism and his temptation in ways that no other character in the story does. We can recite this account as if we know what it is like to be tested by Satan and ministered to by angels. In this case, there is no need to tell our own stories, in our own words, about our wilderness experiences; we can let Mark's story of Jesus speak for us.

At last Jesus becomes a speaker in the story (v. 15) as he emerges from the wilderness to announce that the "time is fulfilled." Jesus now steps into the space in the story left by John's imprisonment. This element of time will loom large as the story unfolds. Mark has already suggested as much with his frequent use of the verbal thread "immediately." This is a clue to the reciter on how to pace the performance. The word *immediately* charges the story with urgency, an intense rhythm that pushes the reciter along. God's invasion of Satan's domain has begun with the coming of God's Son. It is almost as if we do not have time to listen to some carefully developed speeches (as with Matthew's Sermon on the Mount or Luke's Sermon on the Plain) that explain what life in this "Kingdom" will be like. We will see Jesus performing actions that demonstrate that the time is indeed "fulfilled." In fact, Jesus *says* very little in this first chapter, but he *does* a great deal.

The first thing he does is to call some disciples. When someone like Mark gives only a snapshot of information about a character, we pay particular attention to what he *does* give us. We learn that all of the first four disciples are fishermen, that is, part of the peasant class. They are identified as kinsmen. Some family ties are broken as the new community is called into being, and all are called out from their current occupations. The effect is one of disruption and urgency. The scene takes place in Galilee (v. 14), a place to which Mark will bring us again and again. From the "wildness" of the wilderness we have come to the edge of the sea (which for many of Mark's contemporaries was the edge of chaos and uncertainty). Such places are where the new community is established and still resides.

Mark's frequent repetition of the word *nets* presents some intriguing possibilities for oral interpretation and performance. "Casting" and "mending" are actions that suggest some specific descriptive gestures. Mark intermingles words like *catching* and *fishing* to describe the experience of being called into discipleship and mission. When I practiced this section for recital, I began wondering whether the actions of casting, leaving, and mending nets have deeper resonance. What better way to imagine one's own entanglements and attachments in the face of new possibilities than to think of them as "nets"? Jesus arrives and turns such things upside down and inside out.

The scene shifts from natural settings to a traditional time and place for instruction—the synagogue on the Sabbath (v. 21). Here is where Mark reveals another aspect of Jesus' character—his authoritative teaching. I found it very helpful to note how this episode (vv. 21–28) is structured. It is framed by references to the power and authority of Jesus' teaching (vv. 22, 27); in between is an account of Jesus' first exorcism. Jesus' authority to teach and his power to cast out demons are held together in the listener's hearing.

The presence of the "man with an unclean spirit" in the synagogue (v. 23) links this episode with Jesus' previous encounter with Satan and the wild beasts in the wilderness. It is also linked in Mark's gospel to all places where an exorcism will happen. The "unclean spirits" are so pervasive that they have intruded even into the synagogue and must be expelled!

Another of Mark's ironies starts to develop here—the demons that Jesus encounters immediately recognize him as the Son of God; human beings do not, even though they are presented with miraculous wisdom and displays of divine power. Jesus speaks, but only to silence the voice of the one who knows who he is. One choice that the reciter must make is how to say what the unclean spirit says. Are the words spoken in awe? fear? anger? Or is this a taunt? Is the spirit picking a fight? Or is it simply announcing to those in the vicinity who *really* is in their midst? When I perform this passage, I tend to heighten the demon's recognition of who Jesus is, in contrast to others who are puzzling over what is happening. "I *know* who *you* are!" The demon *knows* that Jesus is the enemy of Satan's domain and is absolutely clear about what will happen in the encounter that follows. The demon is outmaneuvered and is powerless in the presence of the "Holy One of God" (v. 24). It can do nothing but what Jesus says.

Setting continues to play an important part in Mark's account as the scene shifts again to the "house of Simon and Andrew" (v. 29). There we meet Simon's mother-in-law, who is sick in bed with a fever. The very first healing story that Mark tells occurs in Simon's own home and among his own family. Yet as the plot develops and Simon's character is disclosed, we will see him have the most difficulty among the disciples in understanding who Jesus is and what Jesus understands his messianic vocation to be. It makes Simon's denial all the more poignant at the end of Mark's gospel.

When I started preparing this part for recital, I was touched by the contrast between synagogue and house. The synagogue was a place where contests happened, a very public setting where Jesus was highly visible. Not so with the house. The word *house* will appear frequently in Mark as a hidden, out-of-the way, marginal place, not worthy of note except through eyes that closely follow Jesus' movements. *House* evokes an appreciation for the mundane and gives attention to that which is ordinary and routine in our everyday lives. Simon's mother-in-law is one of the "little people" who populate Mark's gospel, who make a brief appearance and then leave the story. Mark employs them to exemplify the depth of God's love and concern for those who have no name or status in the existing order. It is most revealing that some of these folks (such as Simon's mother-in-law) are shown to be in need, but also in the role of a servant. Later in the story Jesus will spell out what this means: "Whoever wishes to become great among you must be your servant," and "For the Son of Man came not to be served but to serve" (10:43, 44).

The impact of Jesus' first healing expands from one house to "the whole city [being] gathered together around the door" (1:33). Mark weaves together two aspects of Jesus' authoritative character that he has introduced thus far–healing and exorcism. No teaching happens "around the door." Mark focuses only on these expressions of Jesus' compassion. In recital, I wanted to stress the value of the mood that I believe Mark creates by telling us that it is "evening, at sundown." I believe that the hectic pace that Mark has built up now relaxes a bit, as does the rhythm of the recitation.

The words *evening,* and then *morning* nicely tie these episodes together in the reciter's memory and also in performance. They also link the expressions of Jesus' compassion and power with prayer. I think it is also possible to see this "evening/morning" sequence as a foreshadowing of what will take place on the "evening/morning" of Jesus' arrest and trial. Once again Jesus will be found "in a deserted place" (v. 35), where he will pray (as in 14:36). In chapter 1, Simon is looking for Jesus and finds him praying; in chapter 14, Jesus is looking for Simon and finds him sleeping. In either case, whether by those following Simon or by those who seek Jesus' death, he is "pursued" and "found." Jesus is a character who is frequently "found out" in this narrative by those who are looking for him. Sometimes he is found out against his will (as in 7:24). To my mind, these are examples of the kinds of parallelisms and links in the action that you can find in the entire text, which reinforce the effect and unity of the entire work.

Another example of a parallelism in the narrative structure of the first chapter is between the leper who comes to Jesus (v. 40) and the exorcism that occurred earlier in the chapter. The leper is unclean; the man in the synagogue had an "unclean spirit." Jesus is portrayed as a divine one who squarely faces "uncleanness" and transforms it. Like the "unclean spirit" in the synagogue, the unclean leper seems to recognize who Jesus is and what he has the capacity to do: "If you choose, you can make me clean." We catch a rare glimpse of how Jesus feels when Mark says Jesus is "moved with pity" (v. 41) and that Jesus stretches out his hand and touches the leper. Both the unclean spirit and the leper receive a stern command. Note how differently each responds. The unclean spirit is commanded to be silent; it obeys and comes out. The leper disobeys and talks freely after Jesus warns him to remain silent. Jesus has power over demons that he does not have over human beings. The chapter ends with Jesus' not being able to control either the direction of his movement or human responses to it.

PERFORMING THE TEXT

When I spoke the text on the evening of the NOBS performance, I tried to emphasize the attitude of Mark toward the things he describes. I tried to capture his apparent sense of urgency. The pace of the narrative is quick, and transitions between episodes are short. Yet I believe that Mark does not intend the rhythm of the telling to be so rushed that the listener misses moments of particular intimacy between Jesus and God. For example, I believe that the scene of Jesus' baptism and the account of Jesus' going off "to a deserted place" to pray (v. 35) are places where the reciter can slow down the pace of action for greater emphasis.

It was my responsibility as the first reciter of the evening to awaken the listener's interest by capturing Mark's sense that time is compressed and bursting open with revelation. I compared my responsibility to that of a messenger who rushes onto the stage with a message of utmost importance. Yet it was also my responsibility to lay the groundwork for other performers by emphasizing some of the central themes Mark explores in his gospel. Mark tells us that Jesus is the Son of God and what he will be about throughout the gospel by giving us scenes that demonstrate Jesus' power and special relationship with God. This interaction between plot and theme helps us find the rhythm for the performance of this chapter.

IMPLICATIONS FOR PREACHING AND FOR STUDY

Although the performance of this text did not lead to the composition and performance of a sermon, I have discovered that cultivating the discipline of reciting texts such as the first chapter of Mark feeds the homiletical imagination in the following ways:

- A reciter of a biblical text has to pay close attention to what the text actually says by going over the words again and again in order to internalize them. It helps the preacher experience what is revealed and what is concealed in the language, structure, and organization of a text.
- By standing in the place of the evangelist or biblical author, the reciter distances him- or herself from his or her own world and attempts to identify with the writer's perspective. The preacher takes an important step toward the author's

world by following the author's flow of words and description of actions. Fresh questions, insights, and observations arise when the preacher approaches the text with this level of commitment. For example, deciding *how* to say, "And the Spirit immediately drove him out into the wilderness. He was in the wilderness forty days, tempted by Satan; and he was with the wild beasts; and the angels waited on him" may open up some new interpretations on a brief passage we have heard often (1:12–13).

- By re-presenting the words of a biblical narrator *as if the words were the presenter's own* brings our body and voice more directly into the service of a text. The emotional values expressed in a biblical text such as the gospel of Mark call forth expressive use of bodies and voices. Treating the text as a communicative act enlivens our own communication about that text. For practice, read aloud several times a brief narrative from the first chapter of Mark's gospel (e.g., the baptism of Jesus, vv. 9–11).

Type the passage on a fresh sheet of paper. Arrange the text into memory units or episodes. Now read it over until you can speak the words as if they were your own. As you read, ask yourself the same kinds of questions you asked for reading aloud:

- How does the narrator *feel* about what he is describing?
- How does the narrator want *you* to feel about it?
- What words or phrases bring out this attitude?
- What is God's attitude?
- Even though Jesus does not speak in this part of the story, how do you think he feels about what is happening to him?
- Allow these attitudes to make an impact on how you use your voice. Use your body to create the picture of what is happening. (In fact, try pantomiming the "baptism" itself without using words).
- Make connections with this story by paying attention to your own life story.
- What occasions, events, or anecdotes surface from your experience as you work on this story? Does any of this work generate any ideas for how you might preach on this familiar passage in a fresh way?

Speaking the words of biblical texts *as if* they were your own requires practice, but in the end helps to stimulate new questions, reflections, and oral interpretations of scripture. Not only does it help a text "come alive" in the hearing and experience of a listener; it deepens the level of engagement between the text and its reciter in performance.

In the next chapter I want to awaken the homiletical imagination for preaching by taking a different move. The reciter of a biblical text recognizes that he or she is not the creator of the words that lie on the page. What happens when you turn from being a reciter of the text to being creator of a new story based on the structure, plot, characters, and setting found in the text? This is "oral interpretation" of a different sort—creating new language for a story found in the biblical canon in order to gain a new hearing and interpretation of it.

CHAPTER 5

THE THIRD R: RETELLING STORIES FROM SCRIPTURE

From generation to generation the transmission of the Bible in all its power and vitality has been sensitive to fresh dimensions of meaning to new glimpses of holiness that lie within the text.

WALTER BRUEGGEMANN[1]

I was holding the door open for a student, and after he passed through he thanked me. Then he asked: "Are you the new homiletics professor?" I said that I was.

"Then maybe you can help me. Can you recommend a good book of illustrations to use in my preaching?"

This question comes up a lot with preachers. The short answer is yes, I know of a great many books of illustrations. I also know of scores of resources available by way of the Internet. They are so available, in fact, that I worry that the art and craft of sermon development will soon become more of a cut-and-paste exercise than a work of the human imagination. What that student did *not* ask was: "Should I use this material, and if so, how?" I never got the chance to talk to him about that. Since preaching the gospel is a work arising out of the personhood of the preacher and that preacher's experience of God, I am highly suspicious of cut-and-paste sermons. Imported illustrations or stories too often draw a listener's attention away from their referent and become "free-standing, interchangeable units of experience." Such material suggests that the gospel is so abstract and boring that it needs some sprucing up.[2] What a listener comes to church for is not to hear cut-and-paste sermons. They come to hear a preacher's own witness to the gospel and what implications that has for them and for the enactment and embodiment of faith. I would rather that a preacher catch some of Bruggemann's "new glimpses of holiness" that lie within and emerge from a biblical text than borrow some material to "illustrate" it.

The preacher crafts his or her own witness to the gospel by exercising intelligence, compassion, and imagination. We have seen that engaging a biblical text by means of oral reading or recitation awakens the imagination of both preacher and listener. In this chapter we will see how crafting stories from the perspectives, images, and characters in a biblical text is also a viable and valuable skill in proclamation. All three "Rs" are ways to open up one's life of prayer, ministry, and service to God's creative spirit, which inspires and renews the people of God.

Learning to retell biblical stories takes disciplined, prayerful work that is, admittedly, performed within time constraints. Barbara Brown Taylor once said that we all have the same amount of time; it is how we use it that requires discipline. That student preacher's anxiety about finding good narrative material is certainly understandable. Anyone who preaches week after week knows how difficult it is to keep preaching fresh and engaging. What preacher does not share the same sort of hunger for a good story that would drive the sermon home to the hearer's heart? We would love to learn how to populate our sermons with interesting characters, places, and situations as good stories do. However, given the time pressures preachers are under, the temptation to take shortcuts to a mother lode of narrative material now available in print and on the Internet is great. If we succumb to that temptation too often, we will risk losing our own distinct voice and witness to the gospel. We will start letting others speak for us as if we do not have anything to say for ourselves.

FINDING STORIES THAT SPEAK FROM THE HEART

Once a preacher was taking a workshop that the leader hoped would encourage preachers to exercise their creative imaginations in preaching by developing stories, illustrations, and personal anecdotes. One preacher raised his hand to complain: "Look, I work hard at preparing my homilies. I know how important good preaching is. But where do I get the kind of stories, connections, and illustrations that you are talking about?"[3]

I want to address these two preachers' concerns in this chapter. I propose that "retelling" biblical stories is one way of "finding" stories in ways that will exercise our own imaginations, deepen and expand our engagement with biblical narratives, and enable us to find a form of expression by which we communicate that engagement to our listeners.

In the last two chapters, our focus has been upon mediating the presence of a biblical author by means of reading that scripture aloud or reciting the words "as if" they were our own. In this chapter we will look at the viability of creating and embodying a *new* speaker for a biblical narrative drawn from our own imaginative engagement with the text. We will not do so because we want to debunk or discredit the one who created the biblical narrative or the community that remembered it. We do not want to muffle, but amplify its capacity to speak to us and to our situation. Sometimes our retelling might even come out of a quarrel we are having with the biblical story. If we are to create a new perspective on a biblical story, and find a language and narrative structure of our own to interpret that story for our own listeners, we must be willing to "participate in its struggles, feel its emotions, sense its rhythms, and out of our own loves and hates, fears and hopes, react to its happenings."[4] Creating a new story from our reactions to biblical texts arise from what John Shea calls "the answering imagination."[5] Here are some of the forms the retellings might take:

- Building on the cues that a story's own narrator gives to formulate a new story

- Drawing the listener closer to the perspective of one of the story's "minor" characters
- Going "backstage" of the biblical story's action to find a new angle of vision

This is important work for preachers. Some "old, old stories" are experienced by many as oppressive, violent, or so far removed from our own frames of reference that we do not bother with them. Such stories cry out for fresh, life-giving interpretations. By discovering imaginative ways to retell these kinds of stories (as well as the all-too-familiar ones) we might incite new interest in them. Thomas Troeger puts it this way: Preachers can always "assume there is more to the story" by "imagining that there is more to a biblical story than what we find in the text."[6]

Retelling biblical stories along the lines I suggest is but one form of what is loosely called "narrative" or "story" preaching, a movement that has made an impact on our understanding of preaching for nearly three decades.

RETELLING THE STORY OF NARRATIVE PREACHING

A turn toward story and narrative has been described as a journey that many preachers are choosing to take.[7] Preachers have embarked on these journeys for many different reasons. Many made this move because of their discomfort with didactic preaching in the pulpit. In a didactic sermon, a story, anecdote, or illustration serves the sermon as "evidence" for the idea or theme a preacher is trying to teach. This deductive use of narrative material is a time-honored method of preaching and can be quite effective.

Some preachers, however, began to wonder why their listeners seemed to sit up, pay attention, and respond very differently when a story was told. For example, Eugene Lowry remembers that in his early preaching career he organized sermons as if he were "debating" from the pulpit. That is, "the presentation was deductive in form, with the conclusion announced in the introduction, divided and particularized into the three point body, and then reiterated in the conclusion." To "fill out" his sermons, Lowry added to his library "several volumes of popular anthologies and sermon illustrations."[8]

The kind of didactic, deductive preaching that Lowry described has the following characteristics:

- The goal of preaching is to teach the lessons of the text.
- In order to teach the lessons or meaning of the text the points to be made are abstracted from the text.
- The sermon is aimed primarily at the hearer's mind.
- The sermon is developed in a logical sequential and linear manner.
- The sermon is prepared under the criteria for written material.
- The faith engendered in the hearer is faith that the ideas are true.[9]

The turn that narrative preachers took was away from the pulpit and toward the pews where the listeners were sitting. In 1978, Fred Craddock proposed an "inductive" method that took the listener seriously as a preacher's collaborator in making sense and meaning of the sermon. Craddock's *Overhearing the Gospel* formed the basis for many of the methodological approaches we now call "narrative preaching."[10]

I myself got "hooked" when I discovered that narrative preachers and oral interpreters of texts had a lot in common. Narrative preachers were interested in biblical texts as forms of communication in their own right. They were learning to take the literary form of texts seriously as part of the communicative strategy that an author was using. The form of a text was not simply a "container" that carried a set of ideas or propositions. It was not, they suggested, "an ornamental flourish that can be discarded, but rather is a theological component that could not be ignored."[11]

I thought about how I, when preparing any literary text for performance, had to take the form of that text seriously as an essential element of the originating intelligence presented by means of a text. What was the character of thought, meaning, and effect of the text on the listener within the long history of its interpretation? The text itself was a communicative act, the product of an authorial presence and imagination other than my own. My job in performing was to give the resources of my self and personality to the project of mediating that authorial presence in the performance event. If I were to speak the text from memory or read that text aloud, I had to study the origins of the text and draw some conclusions about its context and the ways it functioned *within* that context. I also had to attend to the intellectual and emotional effect the text had on me when I read and studied it. In performance, I worked to lend the kind of "fullness" or "completeness" that happens when a text is turned into living speech.

I found that I shared an interest with preachers who were trying to understand the ways that texts work as communication *and* theology; that is, narrative preachers were as interested in *how* the text was speaking as in *what* the text was saying. They wanted to allow the biblical text to speak on its own terms and not to treat it as support for their own ideas or as proofs for their points. Just as I was trying to craft performances that honored the literary form they were in and followed the rhetorical cues of their authors, narrative preachers were among those who crafted sermonic forms along the lines that the texts suggested.

Another assumption that performers of texts share with narrative preachers is that listeners are not simply receptors of messages transmitted from speakers. Performers understand that listeners are collaborators in making meaning out of the performance event. Listeners are not simply passive receptors of the information that a performer is presenting; they are participants as the text becomes an event. What happens in performance is that a text that lies silent on the page is transformed into speech and gesture, the *embodied enactment of the 'aesthetic communication'*[12] *of another.* Listeners are essential to "making sense" out of the speech event.

Like narrative preachers, performers of texts spend a great deal of time "listening" to what the text is saying before speaking about it or by means of it to others. In order to craft a performance, one has to "know" the intended audience as well as one can and, throughout the event itself, shape the performance in ways that respond to the cues that a listener will give. Narrative preachers are interested in involving listeners in the preaching event and pay attention to how they respond to sermons that are either punctuated with stories or influenced by narrative modes of communication.

When trying to explain some complicated thought, narrative preachers see that a story or illustration "puts some sweat on"[13] (as Fred Craddock would say) what they are saying. Those who are on their journey toward narrative preaching develop methods for shaping sermons that are built upon these principles.

Some preachers begin with a personal story or anecdote, then move to some scripture or theological theme they want to develop. Some interweave the personal or communal story they know with a story taken from scripture or tradition. Richard Jensen suggests that sermons can be organized by "stitching" a series of stories together, using the narrative structure of the gospel of Mark as an example.[14] Some preachers so completely blur the boundaries between "story" and "sermon" that the sermon itself is constructed as a story. Others blur the boundaries between the preacher and one of the characters in a story by dramatizing one of the characters and speaking in the first person. The recitation of either a long biblical narrative (such as the book of Jonah) or a series of biblical stories (along the lines I suggested in the last chapter) around a theme is a form of narrative preaching.[15] Some narrative sermons need not have narrative material in them at all. Eugene Lowry explains how a sermon might be "story-like," even if there is no story involved: "It began to dawn on me that whether preaching a narrative text or not, in sermonic form I was moving from problem to solution, from itch to scratch, in virtually all my sermons."[16]

It is true that narrative preaching has fluid boundaries and describes a wide variety of approaches in sermon construction and performance. These boundaries are so fluid that I wonder sometimes if narrative preaching can be clearly defined. I once taught a course entitled "Narrative Preaching." When the evaluations came in when the course was completed, the students were still scratching their heads, puzzling over whether there was such a thing as narrative preaching. It was so broadly construed that a single conceptual center was difficult to locate. No student suddenly stood up to announce: "Very well, then, God has convinced me to become a 'narrative' preacher!" Nor did anyone in that class call for a return to purely "doctrinal" sermons that were stripped of story, anecdote, or illustration and aimed solely at explanation and instruction.

We did not discover a clear conceptual center nor some way of neatly describing boundaries between narrative and other kinds of preaching. What we did discover was that "story" has the capacity to teach us different ways to shape our sermons and awaken the intelligent and imaginative engagement of the listener in the preaching event. It can point to new ways to "read" a text and in fact to allow ourselves to be "read" (or addressed) by it on its own terms. We worked at interrogating the stories along the lines suggested in the previous chapters. Then we began to make connections between our own world and the worlds described in the biblical stories. This did not necessarily make us think of ourselves as narrative preachers, but it did finally dispel any lingering notion that stories were useful only as illustration or adornment. They had much more to teach us than that! They teach us that the hunger we have for a good story is part of what makes us human and what makes some of us Christian. We are, as Walter Fisher tells us, *homo narrans,* that is, creatures who give order to their experiences of the world by means of stories and who understand the world as "a set of stories which must be chosen among to live the good life."[17]

For Christians, one primary set of stories we choose as a model for living a good life are those stories that cluster around God's self-disclosure in the life, ministry, and resurrection of Jesus Christ. As people who are baptized in Christ, we bear witness to the suitability of these stories for giving order to our experience, and through that witness we entice others into a relationship with them. We read them aloud to one another, some of us will start developing the skills needed for reciting them, we sing them, and we certainly preach them. We do not always understand them at a first reading, of course, and so we interrogate and study them.

Narrative approaches to preaching also arise out of the fear that biblical stories may be forgotten unless we find fresh ways to present them. When we find ways to let the Bible speak through us as preachers, release it from its moorings in print by transforming it into speech, we can restore its capacity to challenge, interrogate, or confirm our own experiences of being human before God.

In one of his "news reports" from Lake Wobegon, Garrison Keillor was giving an account describing how busy things get in Lake Wobegon around Christmastime. Why do we do all the pageants and concerts and special church services that seem at once so sacred but so silly? "Because it is a great story," he intones again and again, "and we just want to be a part of it."[18] We seek out biblical stories because we long for a relationship with sets of stories that take us out of the narrow "scripts" in which we feel trapped, and expand our awareness of God.

Stories are means by which we humans listen to God; they are also means by which someone listens to us when we speak of God. When we are speaking of God by means of story and storytelling we are "bodying forth"[19] our witness to the presence of God in our lives, in traditions of faithful speech, and in the communities that populate our world. Christians belong to faith communities that sanction the stories of Jesus as stories that constitute and give shape and direction to our lives of prayer, worship, and service. Preaching is but one means by which a preacher weaves together her or his story, the story of the listeners, and the stories received from tradition about God's reconciling action through Jesus Christ. We bear witness to the stories of Christ-with-us because these stories empower and lend coherence to our efforts to "work out [our] own salvation with fear and trembling" (Phil. 2:12b). Thankfully, we are finding different ways to do this because of the work of narrative homiletics.

THE LIMITATIONS OF NARRATIVE PREACHING

Narrative preaching has come into its own, but not without criticism, cautions, and correctives. Some of these reactions are severe. One man recently joined the preaching faculty of a theological seminary believing "the expositional approach to be the most beneficial and legitimate way of proclaiming God's truth."[20] When the president introduced him to the seminary's trustees, the president said: "While others may push such options as narrative and inductive preaching, [he] insists that his students focus on exposition, with its painstaking exegesis, clarifying illustration, and pointed application."[21] Critics have warned that narrative preaching is one sure sign that we have given up on solid exposition and argument in order to heighten the value of sermon-as-entertainment.[22] Some worry that the turn toward narrative preaching masks a new fundamentalism of form, that is, that the only "good" preacher is a "storytelling" preacher. Preachers who do not feel particularly gifted as storytellers may feel marginalized in the rush toward narrative preaching.

The good news is that one's experience of God is more than anyone can express in any given form of human speech. Scott Black Johnston points out that people of faith have developed many different forms of speech to speak of God: "The Bible itself—with its songs, laws, poems, dreams, prayers, and letters—demonstrates that humans have found an abundance of faithful ways to record their experience of God."[23] Why should we be restricted to a the confines of "story" in order to speak of the Holy in the midst of such abundance?

Sometimes we need another kind of speech form because a biblical story does not tell us all that we need to know.[24] For example, once I was taking a communication workshop with some men and women who were working to improve their skills in public speaking. During the course of the workshop I was asked to tell a story. I decided to test the efficacy of some of the principles that I teach in communication courses at the seminary and decided to recite the story of the prodigal son from the gospel of Luke. When I finished my recitation, I sat down and waited for the feedback. One of the participants leaned over to me and asked: "That was a very good story. Did you write it?" At first I thought she was kidding. Then I realized she was quite serious—she had never heard that story before! It was a good example of what William Willimon points out: "I'd claim that in neo-pagan North America the gospel is so odd that at times one must explain it to people, expound it, exposit it, go through it point by point."[25]

Critics such as Willimon remind us that the recitation of a biblical story in a culture that has all but forgotten the Bible has to be placed into a larger chain of interpretive speech. The *sermon* is one of the unique ways that the church has developed to speak of God to the culture in which it lives, and sometimes it cannot do what it has to do by means of a story. Some within and outside our churches have lost the capacity for "thinking in story" because they live lives punctuated by a bewildering series of tragic, unrelated episodes. Others may feel that the story of their lives ended at some point. Memory and experience do not always neatly arrange themselves into plots, but very often appear in our experiences as a series of images and unrelated sensations.[26]

Such situations call us to say clearly and plainly in our sermons *what* we believe and *why* we believe it. Sometimes a story enables us to do that; sometimes other forms of speech are needed. We need to be able to say why we suppose that particular stories are remembered by people of faith and why they matter to us now. Too much reliance on the art of storytelling may make it difficult to speak clearly and plainly to some of our listeners because all of us come to faith in different ways. In any case, biblical stories cannot always speak for themselves—they beg for interpretation and application within listening communities if they are to have resonance, meaning, and life-giving power.

POSSIBILITIES FOR SPEAKING OF THE HOLY BY RETELLING GOD'S STORY

The critics of narrative preaching continue to have their say and offer needed correctives. Narrative modes of thought and preaching need not promise more than they can deliver. People do come to faith differently, often by means of exposition and explanation. The great contribution of narrative preaching is that it has taught us how to think "outside the boxes" we put preaching into by paying attention to ways that people listen. It assumes that human experience tends to be "story-shaped," as is Christian faith itself: "Christianity is defined by the narrative of God's election of Israel and God's continuing faithfulness in the ministry, death, and resurrection of Jesus."[27]

While preaching in narrative modes helps to reach a "story-shaped" listener, it also challenges the dominant stories the culture lives by. Sometimes there is radical dissonance between the stories we live by and that shape our lives and God's Story. God's Story may run counter to our stories more often than not. Some have even tried to justify the oppression of others by invoking elements of God's Story as found in biblical tradition. That is why it is important for preachers to read biblical narratives carefully and critically from the standpoint of prospective listeners in order to find fresh perspectives from which to tell them. In stories, some voices speak and others remain silent. Some characters are at the center of the action while others are on the margins. What happens if we give voice and presence to those who are silent or marginalized by the story?

I want to use three examples of retelling biblical stories to help make my point. The first is in the form of a sermon that I prepared for the Christmas season. As preachers we struggle to find fresh ways of telling that same old story of Jesus' birth from the gospel of Luke. Once, when I was marching through that story again, it occurred to me that (unlike Matthew's gospel) the Luke story gives us very little of Joseph's perspective on the birth of his son. My sermon arose out of this simple question—what would the story sound like if I drew the listener closer to Joseph's point of view?

JOSEPH'S STORY

I think I know you well enough to tell you a secret.
It is a family secret.
It's about the manger scene on the mantel above our
    fireplace.
Our manger scene doesn't have a Joseph in it.
Not a real one anyway.
Several years ago when my in-laws returned from the Holy
    Land,
They brought us the manger scene as a gift.
But when we opened up the box—no Joseph.
Shepherds, wise men, plenty of sheep, baby Jesus,
    Mary…check.
No Joseph!
He must have gotten left behind in some tourist shop in the
    Holy Land.
Or someone, somewhere in the world opened up their
    manger scene
And Mary had suddenly become a bigamist.
Two Josephs!
Not us. We don't have even one.
Now you know. The guy standing in is an understudy,
A shepherd who got lucky.
Joseph is nearly missing in this story too.
Oh, we draw near to Mary when she is singing her song
    about her son.
How could you miss the angels all over the place?
Or the shepherds?

Joseph is harder to spot.

It is also easy to miss the trouble in this story,

With all the singing and praising going on, I mean.

Some of the trouble comes through the place Joseph holds
   in the story.

Joseph, being the village carpenter, liked to have his shop in
   order.

Everything had its place:

Every hammer arranged so he could reach up and grab it at
   the moment he needed it;

Pencils of every shape and size with points finely sharpened
   lying on the table;

Planes hanging neatly against the wall.

There by the door are the axes and saws for cutting the
   wood he worked with.

Yep, if you walked into Joseph's shop, you walked into an
   ordered universe.

Everything there had a purpose in the plan.

Nothing was out of place. That's the way he liked it.

That's the way he needed for it to be.

It was Joseph's business to pay attention to details.

Joseph was a man who carefully studied plans and
   blueprints.

He had to know exact dimensions before he started
   something.

It was his job to be able to know how a house would look
   when it was finished or what the line of the fishing boat
   would be as it cut the water or how the bed would feel
   when you lay down on it.

"You want something done," the elders would say, "take it
   down to Joseph!"

Joseph must have been proud of his reputation.

Now when God stepped into Joseph's world, things started
   to get a little messy.

God has a way of coming into well-ordered lives and
   disrupting them.

First, there was the matter of Mary's pregnancy.

Talk about bad timing!

They weren't even married yet!

Can you imagine the scene where Mary tells somebody like
   Joseph exactly *how* she got pregnant?
From the outset, Joseph's well-ordered universe had to
   stretch.
Joseph had to step aside a little to admit God's spirit into the
   tightly organized workshop of his life.
I hope you will forgive Joseph's silence on the matter.
He doesn't sing as well as Mary does and is not as
   comfortable as she is in the presence of God's growing
   child.
When others ask about it, he's liable to say: "Well, Mary,
   she takes care of the religion for the both of us," then
   he'll leave to go out to the workshop to get ready in his
   own way.
He'll make the best cradle for this baby anybody has ever
   seen.
He'll pick the strongest, sturdiest wood.
It will have the smoothest rockers.
If Joseph could not hold this baby himself, why, this cradle
   would be the next best thing.
As safe, as stable, as secure as Joseph's very own arms.

Then came the announcement of the decree.
Joseph was in his shop working on the design when he
   heard the horses' hooves break the silence in the village
   —a voice that had all of the authority of Rome in it.
Then curses from the villagers as the horses galloped away.
Joseph went to the door and caught a bit of it:
"Why, they'll be asking for our firstborn next!"
"I can't live on what I scrape together now. How am I going
   to pay more tax?"
"I can't afford to pack up and leave now! Who will take
   care of my land, my family? They don't ever think
   about that, do they?"
"Well, I tell you what, this is the last straw for me. This is
   war! I'm not going anywhere and I am not paying
   anything else to Rome! If they want it, they will have to
   come get it off my dead body!"

"What about you, Joseph? What will you do? You going to
     pack up and go all the way down to Bethlehem with
     Mary about due?"
"Don't know," said Joseph. "I'll have to think on it."
Think of Joseph, trying to keep back the panic,
Trying to hold onto the belief that somehow God was in this
     madness.
Then, decisively, deliberately, carefully he says,
"If I leave her here, I might miss the birth. There is nothing
     to do but take her with me. It's not right for a man and
     woman to travel before they're married. But it's not
     right that I should miss this baby being born either.
     Either way it's a mess. It's God's mess. We'll just have to
     hope for the best."
On the day they were to leave, Joseph went into his shop.
He had every intention of putting things back into place.
The hammers were scattered about, the planes lying beside
     the pieces of wood on the floor, the plans and pencils
     on the table, and the cradle out in the middle—in pieces.
He would not be able to finish it before his son was born.
That is when Joseph got angry.
"What kind of a world is this? I am trying to do my best to
     get ready for this child; I am trying to do my part. Now
     I have to take Mary on a ten-day journey. And for
     what? So that I can be enrolled to pay more taxes! My
     ancestors were promised this land by God long ago.
     Now I have to pay taxes to Rome for it? What about
     those promises Mary heard? Why haven't any angels of
     God been coming to visit me? Who will explain it to
     me? Why are these things kept from me? Where is the
     joy in this? What in the world is there for Mary to sing
     about?"

And for the first time in his life, Joseph left his workshop in
     a mess, the pieces of the cradle scattered around the
     floor.
This is the moment when Joseph makes his entrance into
     Luke's story.

"And Joseph also went up from Nazareth in Galilee to Judea
to the city of David, which is called Bethlehem, to be
enrolled with Mary his betrothed, who was with child."

There are many ways to enter God's Story.
There are some, like Mary, who enter it willingly, joyfully,
humbly.
Then there are some like Joseph who enter it angrily,
Through a veil of darkness and danger, with only the
dimmest flicker of a light on the horizon.
There are songs for some, deep disturbing questions for
others.
Then there are some, like Caesar Augustus, who do not
know they have entered it at all.
God is a God who has chosen to see, to hear, and to act
within human history.
God knows the range of human emotion.
God hears with delight the song of Mary.
God sees into the anguished heart of Joseph.
God stands unnoticed in Caesar's palace.
And God is on the long and dangerous road from Galilee to
Bethlehem.
For Joseph it was a journey home.
For Mary it was a journey to a strange place.
So Joseph began to do for her what was so hard for him to do.
Joseph was better at showing than telling.
He was better with his hands than with his voice.
But no matter, as they drew closer and closer, day after day,
the talk turned away from taxes, and homage, and
Caesar and soldiers to talk of home.
Would she have already heard the story of Ruth, Joseph's
kinswoman who had come to Bethlehem as a stranger
long ago to live with her mother-in-law Naomi?
Joseph must have told that one again: how the women of
Bethlehem loved the memory of Ruth, the loving
adopted daughter of the place, the daughter-in-law who
had meant more to Naomi than seven sons.
So God was with them on the journey.

How did they know that God was with them?

Was there be an angel hovering by to protect them?

What was the sign?

Stories. Family stories. Stories of the place. Stories of faith.

Things got busy once they arrived.

So many stories from so many different lives colliding in so
    small a place!

Who would have thought that so many had been born in
    Bethlehem!

And now that his own son was coming there was no more
    room!

No place for him! For Mary! For me!

Disorder! Confusion!

Yet Joseph had an instinct for creating order out of chaos.

His keen eyes were opened, and he knew what to do.

"Over here!" he called and they went toward a stable.

Hay. Warmth. A manger. He looked at the manger.

"It is a good manger. Sturdy. Solid. It will do."

When the baby came, and Mary tenderly wrapped him in
    the tight-fitting clothes of humanity, she noticed the
    manger, but first looked up to Joseph.

He nodded. "It will be all right. It is made well. I made sure
    it was good enough for our son."

There weren't any angels standing by the manger as Mary
    gently laid the baby there.

But there were stories of angels.

The shepherds were just like Joseph.

They would rather show than tell. But they did get the story
    out in halting, nervous voices!

Stories of angels and songs and fields and heaven and sky.

Mary remembered her own story of an angel…but Joseph,

Joseph stepped out for a moment.

Out into the night.

He was a simple carpenter.

He was thinking about that cradle at home.

How he had wanted to do that one thing well for his boy!

How he had hated to leave it unfinished!

Joseph saw no angels in that night sky, but he looked up to
   heaven:
"Thank you," he said. "Thank you for the manger.
It is a good manger.
It is made well.
I made sure before she put him in."
And God knew,
and God understood,
and God wept with Joseph for joy.

That is an example of looking at a familiar story through the
eyes of one of its characters. It means that the preacher creates
and performs a new perspective for the story by looking at a set of
events through new eyes–in this case, through the eyes of Joseph,
a minor character in Luke's story. Notice that I need not develop
"Joseph's Story" by speaking in the first person, as if I were
speaking *as* Joseph. You may not feel that you are skilled at
developing dramatic monologues for performance in worship. You
can tell Joseph's (or any other "minor" character's story) while
maintaining a degree of distance from it. Staying in the third person
is an effective way of freely interweaving story and commentary.

What follows demonstrates a similar approach, except it looks
at a familiar story through the eyes of "God." In Hebrew narratives,
"God" appears as a character who is intimately involved with the
events described. God shows emotion, intervenes, or remains
silent. In the Tower of Babel story (Genesis 11:1–9), there is an
intriguing reference to the complex character of God in verse 7:
"Let US go down" and disrupt the work the people of Shinar are
doing on the tower.

In the retelling of that story which follows, I attempt to amplify
the comic possibilities that the Hebrew narrator suggests by
bringing the listener/reader closer to God's attitude about the
tower-builders' pretension and arrogance. I also tried to come to
grips with the "us" mentioned. How can one "God" be an "us"?
Here is my retelling:

THE DAY GOD CREATED DIFFERENCE

Once upon a time, everybody in the world spoke the same
   language.

And not only did they speak the same language, they all
  looked alike.

They had the same color skin; they wore the same kind of
  clothes; they wore their hair in the same way; and they
  all thought the same thoughts.

But the thought they thought the most was, "*We are special!*"

They lived in a place called Shinar, which was way out in
  the desert.

Well, one day they all got together and decided something.

Since they were so special they would build a city to honor
  themselves.

They would hire the best architects and blueprint makers;
  they would hire the best bricklayers and road builders;
  they would hire the best developers and city planners
  and build this great city.

Now the day after that, the *Shinar Ministerial Association* met
  and decided to build a tower.

A great, great tower up into the heavens

So that anytime they liked, they could climb the tower and
  knock on God's back door!

"Won't God be pleased!" they thought, "and so glad to see US!"

So they went to work on the city and on the tower right
  downtown.

On the weekends the parents would bring their little
  children to gawk at it.

"*Wow!*" said the children, "*What a tower!*"

Now it just so happened that God found out about this.

It happened this way.

God, you see, likes to have friends over from time to time.

God lives in this big chalet that has a great big back porch.

It sits just above the clouds and looks out over all creation.

Every time God's friends come over, they like to go out on
  the back porch after supper. They look at the white and
  wispy carpet of clouds and the cool blue canopy of sky.

"*Wow,*" say God's friends, "*What a creation!*"

One of God's close friends was very, very picky.

This friend was like the person who comes over to your
  house wearing white gloves to find out where you
  haven't dusted.

Some friend! Anyway, this friend came over and after
    supper went out on the back porch with a bad case of
    indigestion.
God's friend was shocked!
Something was poking itself up from underneath the clouds!
"God!" said God's friend, "You better get out here—now!"
God came out with soapy hands and wearing an apron
For it was God's turn to do the dishes.
"What is it?" asked God.
"Look!" said God's friend.
"I don't see anything."
"Don't you see something poking up from under the
    clouds?"
"Where?"
"Over there, over there!"
God went back into the house and returned with God's
    divine binoculars.
"Oh, yes, I see that. Hmmm. Looks like…a tower!"
"A tower? From where?"
God went back inside to look at the divine map.
God came back, looking puzzled.
"It comes from a place called 'Shinar.' I don't remember
    creating a place called 'Shinar'!"
God sighed and said,
"Guess I better go down and see what they're doing. Wanna
    come?"
God's picky friend always went with God on these kinds of
    trips.
So down they went to Shinar, but everybody was so busy
    working that nobody noticed that God was among
    them.
God would ask: "Excuse me, can you tell me about this
    tower project?"
"Don't have time," they'd say. "I'm late to work!"
And they'd move on.
"Boy oh boy," God said, "this tower is really a big deal to
    them."
"It sure is," replied God's friend with a frown. "What are
    you going to do about it?"

God got an idea, then started to laugh.

"What if they all spoke different languages?"

"What? Are you serious?" exclaimed God's friend.

"Yep, as serious as I can be. Want to help?"

Then God's picky friend laughed, "Sure!"

So the next morning, when the men and women showed up
for work on the great tower, they brought with them
their lunch boxes and tools.

One said to the other, "Good morning!"

And another said, "Bon Jour!"

And still another, "Buenos Dias!"

And they all looked at one another suspiciously.

One asked another, "Hand me that hammer!"

But it sounded like gibberish, and he got a hot dog instead.

Another said, "Give me the pail of nails, please?"

But he got a bucket of oatmeal instead.

Still another said, "Hand me that two by four," but got
handed a loaf of French bread.

That was it. A big food fight broke out. The first one in the
world.

Food and tools flew in all directions.

People started grabbing things out of the air.

Some simply took what they had and moved West.

Some took certain tools and went East.

Some took certain foods and went North.

Those that took the grits went South.

Nobody was left to work on the tower, and it was left
unfinished.

But God's work, for that day at least, *was* finished.

Now when God has friends over, God takes them out on
the back porch and says, "Look!"

And they all look and see a rainbow of color, not in the sky,
but in the Earth–different colors of skin and hair and
clothing.

And when God says, "Listen!"

They hear the sounds–different languages spoken, and
songs sung, and stories told.

And God is so pleased and says,
    "Wow, what a creation!"

And on that day, God created difference.
Difference that confounds us to this day, but is a delight
    to God.
And that, dear friends, makes all the difference in the
    world.

These are but two examples of how queries into biblical narratives can prompt fresh retellings of some familiar texts. How might such accounts sound from the perspective of one of the minor characters in the story? Or what happens if we follow the lead of the story's given narrator and work out fuller implications of the biblical narrator's perspective?

In this third and final example, I have tried to take the listener backstage of the story of Jesus' passion and resurrection. Taken together, the stories of Jesus' crucifixion and the events leading up to them are quite dense and complex, especially for children. In the retelling that follows, I try to focus a child's attention (or that of an adult looking through a child's eyes) to three central elements in the passion narratives—the bread, the wine, and the cross. One of the gifts of the art of storytelling is the freedom to allow inanimate objects the power to speak and to endow them with personal traits. We then have the freedom to travel to a different landscape than that which is given in the story. In this story, we go backstage of the gospel accounts in order to see the events from a very different setting than the ones given in the biblical stories.

I first told this story to a group of children on Palm Sunday during children's church. We set a table and arranged on it a cluster of grapes and a cup, a handful of wheat with some bread, some branches cut from a tree, and a cross. Here is the story:

THE LEGEND OF WHEAT, GRAPES, AND WOOD

Once upon a time,
a long, long time ago
(but not so long as you might think),
there was a field outside an ancient city.
And the field was full of wheat,
And when the sun was high in the sky, the wheat looked as
    if it were the very gold of the sun.

On the edge of the field was an arbor where fat, luscious
grapes waited to be plucked.
And around the field was a thicket of woods.
In it, there were trees of all ages, shapes, and sizes.
Some were young saplings who would bend with the wind;
Others were mature oaks that stood defiant and strong;
And still others were ancient and gnarled,
Off to themselves.
One day, while the sun was high in the sky and the field
was golden as the sun,
A stranger came walking into the wheat.
And as he walked, he held out his hands
And caressed the golden tresses of grain.
He walked into the center of the field.
And there he took two handfuls of grain and said to them,
"Oh, Wheat, will you help me?"
And Wheat replied (in a voice that only he could hear),
"What is it that I can do for you?"
"I am going on a long journey," the Stranger said,
"And I will be leaving my friends behind.
Will you help me leave something for them to remember
me by after I am gone?"
And Wheat said,
"You may take whatever you wish."
"Thank you," said the Stranger,
And he left.
Time passed.
And the Stranger returned.
This time the sun was sinking lower in the sky,
And shadows moved across the field.
When the Stranger moved through the heart of the field,
Wheat nodded.
And the Stranger nodded in return.
But it was to the arbor he came.
There he looked up at the ripe, rich fruit and said,
"Oh, Grapes, will you help me?"
And Grapes looked deeply into his eyes and saw sorrow
there. She said,
"What is it that I can do for you?"

Now the Stranger began to pace back and forth through the arbor,
"I am going on a long journey," he said,
"And I must leave my friends behind."
Then he looked up,
"Will you help me leave them something for them to
    remember me by after I am gone?"
And Grapes said in a voice that only he could hear,
"You may take whatever you wish."
And with strong, quick fingers,
the Stranger plucked the fruit from the vine,
And left.
Time passed.
This time when the Stranger returned,
The sun was low in the sky,
And there was just enough evening light left for him to see
    his way into the thicket.
As he passed through the field, Wheat nodded.
As he passed by the arbor, Grapes nodded.
But he did not seem to notice.
He went into the woods,
Past the saplings leaning in the breeze,
Past the oaks standing defiantly against the sky,
And found, in the center of the woods,
A tree, old and gnarled.
For a long time he looked at the old tree.
And for a long time the old tree looked at him.
Finally, the Stranger spoke,
"I have worked with wood all my life.
I can see that you, of all the trees in the forest,
Have what I need."
And the Old Tree spoke.
"I have seen many workers of wood come this way.
Usually they pass me by. What is it that you need of me?"
The Stranger stood still and spoke quietly.
"I am going on a long journey.
At the end of the journey I must do battle with the Great
    Enemy of my friends. Will you supply me with what I
    need for battle?"
The Old Tree was gruff.

"Then you have come to the wrong place. You should have
   stopped by one of the saplings. From one of them you
   could fashion a shaft. On the end of the shaft you could
   place a point, and your spear would fly over a great
   distance and find its place in the heart of your enemy."
The Stranger replied,
"A spear is not what I need."
The Old Tree was puzzled.
"Then you should have stopped by one of the oaks. From
   one of their trunks you could fashion a handle and
   upon the handle you could place a blade. And with
   your sword you could cut down your enemies."
The Stranger replied again,
"A sword is not what I need."
The Old Tree was fearful.
"Then I know why you have come.
You wish to strip me of my old bark, bark that has protected
   me in many storms, and from my bark you desire to
   fashion a shield to protect you from the spears and
   swords of your enemies."
"No," the Stranger said,
"A shield is not what I need."
"You are a strange sort of warrior," whispered the Old Tree,
   "but you have courage and I am old. Very well, you
   may take of me whatever you need."
And with skilled, practiced hands,
the Stranger cut wood from the Old Tree,
and left.
As time passed,
Wheat and Grapes and the Old Tree wondered what had
   become of the Stranger who had come to them.
In the evening they would tell their stories to one another
And share their questions.
One morning,
As the sunlight was beginning to wash over the field and
   drive away the Night,
Wheat looked up and saw the Stranger.
As he walked, he held out his hands and caressed the
   golden tresses.

He came right to the center of the field as he had done
before.

This time, he gathered up the grain and tossed it high in the
sky.

"Thank you, Wheat," he sang out, "for from you I was able
to make bread. Now anytime my friends are hungry for
my presence, they may eat and be satisfied."

He ran for the arbor.

And looking up into the eyes of the Grapes he said, "Thank
you, Grapes, for from you I was able to make drink.
Now anytime my friends are thirsty for my presence,
they may drink deeply and be satisfied."

And he entered into the woods.

When he came to the Old Tree, gnarled, and now scarred
by his hands, he said,

"Bless you, Ancient One,

for from you I was able to fashion beams.

And on those beams I did battle with the fiercest enemy of
us all,

Death.

Whenever Death unleashed its power on me,

You held me up, straight and strong, defiant.

And when my life had ebbed away,

You cradled me in your arms.

When my life returned to me once again,

I looked down and saw that my blood was upon you.

But victory was ours! Death is done! It no longer has
creation in its grip.

Then the Old Tree, gnarled and scarred, spoke to the
Stranger,

"Bless you," he said, "bless you, my friend."

And the Stranger left that place.

But in leaving, left us with the gifts,

Of Wheat, and Grapes, and Wood.

PERSONAL REFLECTIONS ON THE STORY OF NARRATIVE PREACHING

All things [or words] are wearisome;
more than one can express;

the eye is not satisfied with seeing,
> or the ear filled with hearing. (Ecclesiastes 1:8)

These words by an ancient "preacher" might just as well have been scribbled onto a bulletin by someone sitting in church last Sunday. This is the kind of listener that narrative preachers have been trying to reach over the last three decades. They have assumed that such a listener leads a "story-shaped" life and with others in the community of faith, shares a hunger for a good story. Narrative preachers have developed a wide range of methods of incorporating storytelling and story thinking into the composition and performance of their sermons. I have not attempted to do an exhaustive treatment of this wide-ranging methodology, only to expand it further by offering three suggestions:

1. Learn to tell biblical stories from the perspective of a "minor" character.
2. Expand the perspective of a biblical narrator.
3. Go "backstage" of the action in a biblical story to find a different angle of vision.

Although narrative preaching has its critics and its limitations, it has made a strong point: Preachers who ignore the narrative quality of human experience may squander the gift of the listener's presence and participation in the preaching ministry. Practicing forms of narrative preaching also challenges the preacher to enter into a fresh engagement with a biblical story, whether that story be troubling or too familiar.

The suggestions I have made about these forms of preaching build on the assumptions made in previous chapters:

- that "reoralizing" biblical texts by transforming them into expressive speech allows the text to speak in its own voice
- that oral approaches to biblical texts make it necessary to interrogate the text along different lines and raise different sorts of questions and issues than most commentaries
- that out of those questions, new pathways of interpretation open up—not simply for the reading and/or recitation of a text but an imaginative interpretative through a "retelling" of a story

Words can indeed become "wearisome," even oppressive, especially from the pulpit. Yet when we find ways of enlivening our pulpit speech through study, prayer, and imaginative engagement with biblical texts, we incite the listeners' interest in being a part of God's Story. Finding new "glimpses into the Holy" will help us speak of it more fully, creatively, and passionately.

CONCLUSION

New technologies of communication are shaping the many ways we listen for and speak of the Holy; they have awakened our appetites for the oral and the visual, for the coalescence of image and idea, for spontaneity, for emotion and energy. The technologies have developed so rapidly that we have scarcely had time to think about the capacity of printed words to form our language for prayer and proclamation. We wonder what competencies are needed to speak of the Holy during the seismic shift from a print culture to an electronic media age. Since our culture appreciates the values of *oral* communication, what is the place of print? How do we speak from the pages our literary traditions have left us?

I have attempted to address these matters in this book. Some forms of worship that are being developed for use in an electronic culture devalue the medium of print. Projection screens are making hymnals, books of worship, and bulletins unnecessary or at least highly suspect. Pulpits, pews, and other artifacts of print culture are slowly being removed from "contemporary" worship spaces. Those who speak from manuscripts are greeted with sighs and groans unless they speak as if the manuscript is not there. There are signs everywhere that the printed word will no longer be the dominant medium for facilitating worship. This causes many to worry about the future of "traditional" worship. They cling to cherished books and paper as if they were lifelines to the presence of God. Others celebrate the dismantling of print culture and the forms of discursive speech that it spawned. Most of us are stranded somewhere in between.

I do not believe that the printed word will disappear altogether from communal worship. The history of media shows that when new technologies are developed, they do not displace existing ones but assimilate and build on them. I believe that new forms of worship will not only include but will further develop the ways we employ the printed word and speak from the pages of our biblical and liturgical traditions. There will always be someone standing in worship who will speak in a space *between* the printed texts, the electronic images, and the oral traditions and interpretations that bear the marks of "God-with-us." That someone, however—whether that person is in the role of preacher, lector or presider—will need to cultivate the kinds of skills that are valued for oral communication. Listeners will become increasingly impatient with speakers who do not seem to understand what they have been given to read aloud. They will not pay attention to a speaker whose eyes never leave a page, whose energy level is low, whose pace is plodding, and whose vocal tone is monotonous. Nor will they trust a speaker whose manner of speaking seems "packaged" for television. "Slick," stylized, or affected speakers may help us to more efficiently move through our worship, but they will not seem authentic to us. Effective preachers and other speakers of the Holy in worship will come to learn

- to cultivate practices of placing oneself before God and communicating with God through prayer and service
- to understand worship as *aesthetic* communication that fully engages our emotions, senses, and intellects
- to treat biblical and liturgical texts as forms of utterance that address both speakers and listeners
- to treat the voices in scripture as "companions" that become present to listeners in forms of embodied proclamation
- to release those voices in scripture (and those marginalized by them) through the three Rs of reading, reciting, and retelling

Performance studies is a rich resource for helping us understand the communicative values of scripture and sermon in worship. It is a discipline of inquiry that

- teaches that human beings are *natural* performers (in the best sense of that word) whose everyday lives are punctuated with the performances of roles and rituals

- describes how the communicative elements of language and form coalesce with speech, gesture, and embodiment in worship and preaching
- teaches that a biblical text can be transformed into a lively form of speech

We need not shy away from the language and concepts of performance theory to develop a theology of proclamation. One of the central metaphors of the Christian faith is also an efficacious one in performance theory. In speaking a text, a performer offers thought, voice, and body to the abstract words printed on a page in order to give them life as human utterance. Christians affirm Jesus of Nazareth to be the Christ, the embodied Incarnate Word of a Holy God. In obedience to God, Jesus disclosed and embodied a way of being present before God and one another in his own time and for all time to come.

Much of Jesus' teaching that the church remembers is in the form of "little dramas" in which a listener vicariously participates, parables and stories that present the claim of God's grace on human life. Even the story of Jesus itself (as remembered by the four gospel writers) can be imagined as a drama of redemption that includes and implicates all who would attend to it. Christians perform their best understanding of the Word in life and worship or find themselves standing against it.

The word *drama* describes a set of practices that many churches are adopting as part of their communal worship. Dramatic monologues, skits, plays, and Christian theater groups abound in "media-friendly" churches. *Drama* is not only a genre of aesthetic communication but also a useful metaphor that surfaces in performance theory. It describes the complex field of human relationships. We are all "social actors" who play out our roles in everyday life lived before God and one another. We also recognize how the performances we enact in everyday life are linked with performances we see played out on a stage.

My emphasis in this book has been on the use of drama as a metaphor for understanding dimensions of meaning proclamation and worship. Released from its pejorative uses, the word *drama* opens up our interpretation of the preaching event and suggests the following directions for growth and development:

Learning to read scripture aloud with understanding and affect is to overcome the strange silence of the Bible in everyday life and in corporate worship. Practicing time-honored conventions of oral interpretation of literature allows voices of scripture to speak freshly of the Holy. A text bears the marks of authorial presence that, when embodied in performance, becomes a living voice in the assembly. Voiced and embodied texts are subject to interrogation. They can also speak to us of the *hunger* for the Holy and the ongoing need for God's self-disclosure through processes of interpretation. Developing an *oral* hermeneutic, that is, a form of interpretation that takes seriously the *orality* of scripture, means changing the kinds of questions we ask of texts and expanding the parameters of our imagination and perceptions.

An effective recitation of a biblical narrative closes the distance between the world of the listener and the world of the story. When the performer of a biblical narrative speaks the words of the text *as if* they are the performer's own, the action of the biblical story becomes more immediate to the experience of the listener. Abstract words from another, distant time return to the oral culture of stories, memory, proverbs, aphorism, and humor. Writers and editors helped preserve the memory of the event; a reciter who speaks the story with understanding and feeling restores the quality of the story as an event within the shared experience of a community. A biblical narrative in performance is an opportunity for both the reciter and the listener to connect their own stories with the stories remembered by the earliest followers of Jesus and his disciples. It can also raise questions that evoke other stories for proclamation.

Oral hermeneutics and conventions of oral performance open new windows in the imaginations of both preachers and listeners. The questions that arise from my oral interpretation of biblical stories prompt the creation of my *own* "biblical" story. One form for presenting biblical narratives is to allow the language, attitude, and thought of that story to *come through* in my own recitation. Another is to draw from my imagination and experience to create a new story in response to the biblical one. *What we give to the story is a new future by amplifying its capacity to speak of the Holy in our time and place.*

Narrative homiletics developed from the conviction that human beings are hungry for stories. Although each one of us listens and learns in different ways, it is clear that we humans *are* creatures who tell stories. We live in a sea of story in our electronic culture, and we consume stories as quickly as they are produced. In fact, we are constantly tempted to displace our own stories with other more sensational ones we borrow from print or electronic sources. Where are we to find those stories wherein we can hear echoes of the Holy? For many the biblical stories have become too remote or even too repressive. Most biblical stories are limited in their capacity to speak for themselves, and they require interpretation. As Christians we practice disciplines of prayer, worship, interpretation, and performance that help us forge connections between God's stories and our own. These intersections become fertile ground for retelling the stories we hold in our memories. Three Rs—reading, recitation, and retelling—press scripture to move more deeply into the recesses of our own lives and imaginations. Yet they press us to move together toward the future that God has in mind for us. It is a future charged with hope, the hope for a new hearing.

EPILOGUE

"God is spirit, and those who worship [God] must worship in spirit and truth."

JOHN 4:24

Since I began this book with a memory of a church, I will close with a memory of another. The two churches are similar in some respects. Both were built at about the same time by farmers who wanted a place of worship close by. Both structures are small, plain, and unadorned. One sits in a cornfield; the other sits in a neighborhood that was once a cornfield. Yet one is empty and silent, and the other is filled with noise. In the first, the Spirit of God is blowing old relics of worship about in a breeze; in the other, the Spirit is blowing through as music, song, and speech. Both have the patina of age, yet the lively one is doing what it has always done, but has found ways of doing it well. That has been the dominant note I have tried to play in this book—that we need not abandon altogether the traditional ways of speaking and reading in worship, though the temptation to do so is strong. New electronic technologies can be assimilated into our worship, but need not eclipse it. The new media do, however, press us toward lively speech, but speech that is credible, believable, and congruent with our personalities. Speaking wisely and well means

- cultivating a spirituality of presence
- taking seriously the orality of scripture through study, reading, and recitation

- finding new and imaginative ways of retelling the stories of scripture

I park the car and I am already hearing the tolling of the 150-year-old church bell. Mitch, the pastor, always asks one of the children if they want to open the service in this way, and there is no shortage of volunteers! I walk inside and take one of the few places left on one of the refurbished benches that have been here from the beginning. Several latecomers are content to stand near the old windows or even sit on the floor. The Spirit is invoked by the pianist, a jazz musician whom Rev. Mitch knows. Although he has no formal training as a "church musician," he creates simple, musical congregational responses, plays a mean accompaniment to the hymn singing, and has put together an intergenerational choir.

Around me are people whom I have met only recently. I have learned from previous conversations that many are returning to church after a long absence. Some are from interfaith marriages; others are alienated from their denominational roots. When I ask them at coffee hour why they come, they can only answer: "I had almost given up on church but something draws me here. I can't really explain it." (Perhaps they are, like the speaker in Wallace Stevens' poem "Sunday Morning," prompted by the Spirit to make the journey "over the seas, to silent Palestine, dominion of the blood and sepulchre" to see if the rumors of resurrection are still true?)

Rev. Mitch leads us through the service. His hair and beard are white and long (like those of the Ancient of Days we once imagined as children), but a smile is no stranger to his face. He is robed and vested and instead of a pulpit to hold his notes for reading and preaching, he carries an old, stressed-leather folder with faded ribbons he uses as markers. The folder frees him to be mobile, and he moves freely and purposefully before and among the congregation. Though Mitch does not have a "trained" speaking voice, he reads the biblical texts clearly and with energy and conviction.

Mitch and I have discussed his preaching ministry over several lunches. His imagination for preaching is facile, and his interpretations of biblical texts are fresh. He feels, however, that his sermons are too "wordy" and "essay-like," so he is trying to extend his grasp of narrative modes of preaching and to practice writing in an oral style. I have made some suggestions along some lines I have outlined in this book, namely,

- that he develop an *oral* study of the scriptures by reading them aloud and noting how inflection, thought, and attitude create new shades of meaning and avenues for exploration
- that he set some realistic goals for committing portions of the scripture to memory for use in reading, preaching, or presiding in worship
- that he try to tell a biblical story either by developing different perspectives on the events described or by expanding on perspectives already given in the text

Today he has asked me to attend and to listen as he tries something new.

At the center of the sermon is a character Mitch has created. We will see the events recorded in the biblical text through her eyes. Her name is Rachel, and she is waiting with her mother along the main road through Jericho. Her mother expects someone named Jesus to come that way, but Rachel is interested in something (or someone!) else. Someone is sitting up in a sycamore tree! She keeps trying to get her mother's attention to show her but her mother is too busy looking for the prophet.

Rachel recognizes the man. He is the one who comes from time to time to collect taxes. Every time he leaves, her mother is in tears and her father sits in silence with an angry look on his face. So it is that angry look she shows to him. He doesn't see it. He is looking in the same direction her mother is.

Then there is a sound, a murmuring in the crowd, a "Here he comes!" and then general shouts of enthusiasm. The man named Jesus is with some others who are following behind him. They seem to enjoy the attention, but Jesus is simply standing in the middle of the road, looking up into the tree. At first it looks as if Jesus is making fun of him (he has a name that is hard to spell, much less to pronounce: Z-a-c-c-h-a-e-u-s!) Others are laughing at the little tax collector up in the tree. But not Jesus. He seems very friendly toward the man whom everyone loves to hate. Next thing she knows, Zack-what's-his-face is climbing down out of the tree and is leaving the scene with Jesus. People are left grumbling and scratching their heads.

A few days later, Rachel sees the man come up to the house. And after he leaves, her mother is crying again, but the crying is very different this time. And the look on her father's face is different too. It is a look of happiness, not of anger! He is holding up a bag (a heavy bag, it looks like) full of coins! "Four times? Four times as much?" her father is saying, and now she sees her father and her mother holding each other tightly and motioning for Rachel to come close to them for a "family hug."

What happened to old what's-his-face? She is left wondering. And what happened to Jesus? What happened *between* them? She'd have to think about that for a long time.

And so would we, said Mitch. We are left wondering what would happen if we were to give generously. Would that help us understand what happened between Zacchaeus and Jesus? Be careful if you look hard for Jesus. He might just invite you into his work, into his heart, and into his love.

Later that afternoon, we are sitting in the church. Everyone else has gone home and we have returned after lunch. We have talked about the sermon and how well I felt he met his goals. Now I ask him to tell me how he came to be the part-time pastor here. He is a psychotherapist by training and has an active and extensive practice. Why take this on? I wanted to know.

One of those smiles comes home to his face. "I missed preaching and leading worship," he explains. "When the pastor left here, he left thinking that the church was dying. So they called me to see if I might help them out—to decide whether to live or to die. They were just a very small core group of people who had been here for years. They didn't know what to do."

"So what happened?" I asked. "Why didn't it die?"

"I told them that they didn't *have* to die. That this was a marvelous space and could become a lovely place to worship God in this neighborhood. But we'd have to work at it and hope that the Spirit blew back in."

So that is what they did. First, *they enlivened the space.* They removed some of the old relics, such as the faded red carpet and the cushy furniture that crowded the chancel. The open space up front would now be available for flowers, the baptismal font, and the choir. They would move the table to a prominent spot and plan to celebrate communion every week. They refurbished the original wooden floors and the benches that I and the others sat on—if we were lucky! They restored the old bell and its rope to good working order and "dressed" the space with colorful textures and candlesticks.

Next, Mitch worked to *enliven the music and modes of liturgical speech.* The piano was tuned to the jazzman's satisfaction, and his talent drew out new talent—people in the community came who loved to sing in the choir. Mitch trained those who wanted to read aloud in worship and worked on his own reading and preaching.

Finally, Mitch and the congregation attempted to *enliven their own understanding of who Jesus Christ is for us today.* At the center of worship was table fellowship. When Mitch (or another representative of the congregation) stood to welcome those assembled to worship and specifically to come to the table, they professed their belief that Christ was doing the inviting and that Christ offered himself to all who would come. Christ was present to all those who came, regardless of their measure of belief or disbelief, regardless of their background or levels of understanding.

Now we had to get down to business. We had to plan the worship together. Mitch would be out of town, and I was to be the preacher and worship leader. Mitch asked me what text I wanted to preach on. "I would like to pick up where you left off today," I said. "What comes after the story of 'Zack-what's-his-face'?"

We looked, and there was the parable of the ten pounds (Lk. 19:11–27), an account of servants who are given something and make something out of what they are given, to the delight of the one they serve. I looked at Mitch and let go of a little laugh—"I think I can do something with this one."

And so can we all. We take the "ordinary" things we have been given—the language and structure of story, the language of everyday speech, our experiences in prayer and study, the performances in everyday life in which we are witnesses or actors, a few words lifted from a page from the bible or book of worship, and we make what we can out of them—with the help of the Spirit of God.

NOTES

Introduction

[1]Philip Larkin, "Church Going," in *The Norton Anthology of Poetry,* ed. Arthur M. Eastman et al. (New York: Norton, 1970), 1148; reprinted from Philip Larkin, *The Less Deceived* (Hessle, East Yorkshire, England: Marvell Press, 1955).

[2]Michael J. DeVito, "Presidential Style: An Historical Perspective" in *Reading, Preaching and Celebrating the Word,* ed. J. Paul Marcoux (Palm Springs, Fla.: Sunday Publications, Inc., 1980), 94–102.

[3]Ibid., 95.

[4]Larkin, "Church Going," 1148.

[5]David L. Bartlett, "Story and History: Narratives and Claims," *Interpretation* 45:3 (July 1991): 229.

[6]Carol Simpson Stern and Bruce Henderson, *Performance: Texts and Contexts* (New York and London: Longman, 1993), 9.

[7]Elizabeth Achtemeier, *Preaching as Theology and Art* (Nashville: Abingdon Press, 1984), 52.

[8]Alla Bozarth-Campbell, *The Word's Body: An Incarnational Aesthetic of Interpretation* (Tuscaloosa, Ala.: The University of Alabama Press, 1979), 136–44.

[9]Georges Gusdorf, *Speaking (La Parole),* trans. and with an intro. by Paul T. Brockelman (Evanston, Ill.: Northwestern University Press, 1965), 56.

[10]E. Y. Mullins, *Baptist Beliefs* (Philadelphia: Judson Press, 1925), 12.

[11]Donald Juel, "The Strange Silence of the Bible," *Interpretation* 51:1 (January 1997): 5.

[12]James D. Smart, *The Strange Silence of the Bible in the Church: A Study in Hermeneutics* (Philadelphia: Westminster, 1970).

[13]Juel, "Strange Silence," 5.

[14]Ernesto Cardenal, "The Cosmos Is His Sanctuary (Psalm 150)," trans. Donald D. Walsh, in *Modern Poems on the Bible: An Anthology,* ed. and with an intro. by David Curzon (Philadelphia and Jerusalem: The Jewish Publication Society, 1994), 297.

[15]Larkin, "Church Going," 1148.

Chapter 1: What Communication Means for Preaching and Proclamation

[1]James W. Carey, "A Cultural Approach to Communication," *Communication* 2 (1975): 16.

[2]Peter S. Hawkins, "Henry Ward Beecher and Communication at Yale in the 1990s," *Reflections* (Summer-Fall 1991): 11.

[3]Carey, "A Cultural Approach to Communication," 6.

[4]James W. Carey, "Communication and Culture," *Communication Research* (April 1975): 188.

[5]Pierre Babin with Mercedes Iannone, *The New Era in Religious Communication,* trans. David Smith (Minneapolis: Fortress Press, 1991), 71.

[6]Paul A. Soukup, *Communication and Theology: An Introduction and Review of the Literature* (London: WACC, 1983), 27.

[7]M. R. Chartier, *Preaching as Communication* (Nashville: Abingdon Press, 1981), 15.

[8]Ronald J. Pelias, *Performance Studies: The Interpretation of Aesthetic Texts* (New York: St. Martin's Press, 1992), 16.

[9]Fred Craddock, *Preaching* (Nashville: Abingdon Press, 1985), 122–23.

[10]See also on this point Charles L. Bartow, *The Preaching Moment: A Guide to Sermon Delivery* (Nashville: Abingdon Press, 1980), 13–20.

[11]Susan D. Newman, "Preaching to Baby Boomers" in *Preaching on the Brink: The Future of Homiletics,* ed. Martha J. Simmons (Nashville: Abingdon Press, 1996), 43.

[12]Babin and Iannone, *The New Era,* 81.

[13]Pelias, *Performance Studies,* 6

[14]Soukup, *Communication and Theology,* 28.

[15]Pelias, *Performance Studies,* 7.

[16]I am referring to a quote by W. J. Beeners in Bartow, *The Preaching Moment,* 19.

[17]For further reference on this point see Jonas Barish, *The Anti-Theatrical Prejudice* (Berkeley: The University of California Press, 1981) and Christine Catharina Schnusenberg, *The Relationship Between the Church and the Theatre* (New York: The University Press in America, 1988).

[18]David Buttrick, *Homiletic: Moves and Structures* (Philadelphia: Fortress Press, 1987), 334.

[19]Elizabeth Achtemeier, *Creative Preaching: Finding the Words* (Nashville: Abingdon Press, 1980), 29.

[20]Quintilian, *Institutio Oratoria,* trans. H. E. Butler, vol. 3, bk. 9 (Cambridge, Mass.: Harvard University Press, 1921), 391.

[21]Haddon W. Robinson, *Biblical Preaching: The Development and Delivery of Expository Messages* (Grand Rapids: Baker, 1980), 207.

[22]Peter Lucas Senkbeil, "Faith in Theatre: Professional Theatres Run by Christians in the United States and Canada and Their Strategies for Faith-Art Integration" (Ph.D. diss., Northwestern University, 1995).

[23]Tom F. Driver, "Drama: An Expression of the Kerygma," *Union Seminary Quarterly Review* 9:1 (1953): 14.

[24]E. Winston Jones, *Preaching and the Dramatic Arts* (New York: The Macmillan Company, 1948), 16, 19.

[25]Hawkins, "Henry Ward Beecher," 14.

[26]Tom F. Driver, *The Magic of Ritual: Our Need for Liberating Rites that Transform Our Lives and Our Communities* (San Francisco: HarperSanFrancisco, 1991), 88.

[27]Gordon W. Lathrop, *Holy Things: A Liturgical Theology* (Minneapolis: Augsburg Fortress Press, 1993), 214.

[28]Richard Schechner, *Performance Theory,* rev. ed. (New York and London: Routledge, 1988), 120.

[29]Peter Brook, *The Empty Space* (New York: Atheneum, 1968), 52.

[30]Ibid., 49.

Chapter 2: Speaking and Hearing a "Lively Word"

[1]From the Foreword to Thich Nhat Hanh, *Living Buddha, Living Christ* (New York: Riverhead Books, 1995), xiii.

[2]See Jana Childers' excellent treatment of this subject in *Performing the Word: Preaching as Theater* (Nashville: Abingdon Press, 1999), 57–77.

[3]See G. Robert Jacks, *Getting the Word Across: Speech Communication for Pastors and Lay Leaders* (Grand Rapids: Eerdmans, 1995).

[4]Clyde Fant, *Preaching for Today,* rev. ed. (San Francisco: Harper and Row, 1987). See especially chapter 10, 159–76.

[5]Professor Wardlaw worked from this premise in a teaching session I observed in a workshop held through the auspices of McCormick Theological Seminary in Chicago, Illinois, in June 1988.

[6]Rebecca Chopp, *Saving Work: Feminist Practices of Theological Education* (Louisville: Westminster John Knox Press, 1995), 76.

[7]Hans-Ruedi Weber, *The Book That Reads Me: A Handbook for Bible Study Enablers* (Geneva: World Council of Churches Publications, 1995), 4.

[8]From Gabriel Fackre's lecture, "Sound Doctrine in the Church," The Frederick Louis Trost, Jr., Lectures, presented at St. Paul's United Church of Christ, St. Paul,

Minn., October 18, 1992, and at the United Theological Seminary, New Brighton, Minn., October 19, 1992.

⁹Evans Crawford, *The Hum: Call and Response in African-American Preaching* (Nashville: Abingdon Press, 1995): 18–19.

¹⁰Alan Jones, *Sacrifice and Delight: Spirituality for Ministry* (New York: Harper, 1992), 50.

¹¹H. E. Luccock, *In the Minister's Workshop* (Nashville: Abingdon-Cokesbury, 1944), 193.

CHAPTER 3: THE FIRST R: READING YOUR TEXT

¹Paul Gray and James Van Oosting, *Performance in Life and Literature* (Boston: Allyn & Bacon, 1996), 2.

²Harvey H. Guthrie, "Anglican Spirituality: An Ethos and Some Issues" in *Anglican Spirituality,* ed. William J. Wolf (Wilton, Conn.: Morehouse-Barlow, 1982), 9.

³Lynn C. Miller, "The Study of Literature in Performance: A Future?" in *The Future of Performance Studies: Visions and Revisions,* ed. Sheron J. Dailey (Annandale, Va.: National Communication Association, 1998), 10.

⁴Charlotte Lee, *Oral Reading of the Scriptures* (Boston: Houghton Mifflin Company, 1974), v.

⁵S. S. Curry, *Vocal and Literary Interpretation of the Bible* (New York: Macmillan, 1903), 22.

⁶Ronald J. Pelias, *Performance Studies: The Interpretation of Aesthetic Texts* (New York: St. Martin's Press, 1992), 7.

⁷Dwight Conquergood, "Beyond the Text: Toward a Performative Cultural Politics" in *The Future of Performance Studies: Visions and Revisions,* ed. Sheron J. Dailey (Annandale, Va.: National Communication Association, 1998), 26.

⁸See especially Charles L. Bartow's extensive and richly funded work on this, *God's Human Speech: A Practical Theology of Proclamation* (Grand Rapids, W. B. Eerdmans, 1997).

⁹Thomas Boomershine, "Jesus of Nazareth and the Watershed of Ancient Orality and Literacy," *Semeia* 65 (Atlanta: Scholars Press, 1994): 8.

¹⁰Conquergood, "Beyond the Text," 26.

¹¹William H. Pritchard, *Frost: A Literary Life Reconsidered* (New York: Oxford University Press, 1984), 60.

¹²Charles L. Bartow, *Effective Speech Communication in Leading Worship* (Nashville: Abingdon Press, 1988), 21.

¹³Pierre Babin with Mercedes Iannone, *The New Era in Religious Communication,* trans. David Smith (Minneapolis: Fortress Press, 1991), 71.

¹⁴Tom F. Driver, *The Magic of Ritual: Our Need for Liberating Rites That Transform Our Lives and Our Communities* (San Francisco: Harper, 1991), 81.

¹⁵Leander Keck, "The Pre-Modern Bible in the Post-Modern World," *Interpretation* 50:2 (April 1996): 130.

¹⁶Mary Catherine Hilkert, *Naming Grace: Preaching and the Sacramental Imagination* (New York: Continuum, 1997), 16.

¹⁷Clark M. Williamson and Ronald J. Allen, *A Credible and Timely Word: Process Theology and Preaching* (St. Louis: Chalice Press, 1991), 120–25.

¹⁸Ellen Davis, *Imagination Shaped: Old Testament Preaching in the Anglican Tradition* (Valley Forge, Pa.: Trinity Press International, 1995), 263.

¹⁹Keck, "The Pre-Modern Bible," 138, 135.

²⁰Davis, *Imagination Shaped,* 250.

²¹I am indebted to Charles L. Bartow here. See his article, "In Service to the Servants of the Word: Teaching Speech at Princeton Seminary," *The Princeton Seminary Bulletin* 13:3 (1992): 275–76.

²²Herman Cohen, *The History of Speech Communication: The Emergence of a Discipline, 1914–1945* (Annandale, Va.: Speech Communication Association, 1994), 98. Cohen is

citing an essay by R. L. Lyman, "Oral English in the High School," *Quarterly Journal of Public Speaking* 1 (1915): 241–59.

[23]Curry, *Vocal and Literary Interpretation*, 22.

[24]Pelias, *Performance Studies*, 47.

[25]Carol Simpson Stern and Bruce Henderson, *Performance: Texts and Contexts* (New York: Longmans, 1993), 3.

[26]Nicholas Lash, *Theology on the Way to Emmaus* (London, SCM Press, 1986), 42.

[27]Ibid.

[28]Johan Huizinga, *Homo Ludens: A Study of the Play Element in Culture* (Boston: Beacon, 1955), 13.

[29]Stern and Henderson, *Performance*, 184.

[30]Ibid., 263.

[31]George Steiner, *Real Presence* (Chicago: The University of Chicago Press, 1989):137–64.

[32]J. Paul Marcoux, "The Bible as Literature: An Experiential View" in *Reading, Preaching, and Celebrating the Word*, ed. J. Paul Marcoux (Palm Springs, Fla.: Sunday Publications, 1980), 6.

[33]Keck, "The Pre-modern Bible," 137.

[34]Ronald J. Pelias, "Schools of Interpretation Thought and Performance Criticism," *Southern Speech Communication Journal* 50 (Summer 1985): 353.

CHAPTER 4: THE SECOND R: THE RECITATION OF SCRIPTURE

[1]Thomas E. Boomershine, *Story Journey: An Invitation to the Gospel as Storytelling* (Nashville: Abingdon Press, 1988), 19.

[2]Quote found on the Network of Biblical Storytellers (NOBS) Web site at www.nobs.org in August 2001.

[3]Hans-Ruedi Weber, *The Book that Reads Me: A Handbook for Bible Study Enablers* (Geneva: World Council of Churches Publications, 1995), 2.

[4]Walter Ong, S.J. "Text as Interpretation: Mark and After," *Semeia* 39 (Summer 1987): 7.

[5]The definitive book that outlines this approach is Boomershine, *Story Journey*.

[6]In Norma Reitz and Sandra Livo, *Storytelling: Process and Practice* (Littleton, Colo.: Libraries Ltd., 1986), 95, 119–26, the authors use the term *paralinguistic devices* to identify the score of expressive vocal and physical behaviors that help a speaker realize and interpret a text.

[7]David Rhoads, "Performing the Gospel of Mark" in *Body and Bible: Interpreting and Experiencing Biblical Narratives*, ed. Bjorn Krondorfer (Philadelphia: Trinity Press International, 1992), 104.

[8]Boomershine, *Story Journey*, 24, 27.

[9]Mark Allen Powell, *What is Narrative Criticism?* (Minneapolis: Augsburg Fortress Press, 1990), 9.

[10]Ibid., 20.

CHAPTER 5: THE THIRD R: RETELLING STORIES
FROM SCRIPTURE

[1]Walter Brueggemann, *The Bible Makes Sense* (Winona, Minn.: St. Mary's College Press, 1978), 10.

[2]Richard A. Lischer's "Response" to Scott Black Johnston in "Who Listens to Stories: Cautions and Challenges for Narrative Preaching," *Insights: The Faculty Journal of Austin Seminary* (Spring 1996): 29.

[3]Attributed to Robert P. Woznak, "The Preacher and the Poet," *Worship* 60:1 (January 1986): 47.

[4]Gilbert L. Bartholomew, "Human Encounter in the Spiritual Gospel," *Worship Alive* (Nashville: Discipleship Resources, n.d.): n.p.

[5]John Shea, *Spirit Master* (Chicago: The Thomas More Press, 1987), 201.

[6]Thomas H. Troeger, *Ten Strategies for Preaching in a MultiMedia Culture* (Nashville: Abingdon Press, 1996), 22–29.

[7]See especially Wayne Bradley Robinson, ed., *Journeys Toward Narrative Preaching* (New York: Pilgrim Press, 1990).

[8]Eugene Lowry, "The Narrative Quality of Experience as a Bridge to Preaching," in Robinson, *Journeys,* 68.

[9]Richard A. Jensen, *Telling the Story: Variety and Imagination in Preaching* (Minneapolis: Augsburg, 1980), 27.

[10]Fred B. Craddock, *Overhearing the Gospel* (Nashville: Abingdon, 1978).

[11]Scott Black Johnston, "Who Listens to Stories: Cautions and Challenges for Narrative Preaching," *Insights: The Faculty Journal of Austin Seminary* (Spring 1996): 8

[12]See Ronald J. Pelias, *Performance Studies: The Interpretation of Aesthetic Texts* (New York: St. Martin's Press, 1992), 12, 15.

[13]This is an expression Craddock frequently uses in his teaching and conversations about preaching.

[14]Richard A. Jensen, *Thinking in Story: Preaching in a Post-Literate Age* (Lima, Ohio: C. S. S. Publishing, 1993), 109ff.

[15]See especially Gilbert L. Bartholomew, "Narrative Preaching," in *Worship Alive* (Nashville: Discipleship Resources, n.d.): n.p.

[16]Lowry, "The Narrative Quality of Experience as a Bridge to Preaching," 72.

[17]Walter R. Fisher, "Narration as a Human Communication Paradigm: The Case of Public Moral Argument," *Communication Monographs* 51 (March 1984): 6.

[18]From the broadcast of "A Prairie Home Companion," on December 12, 1999.

[19]I am indebted to Charles L. Bartow for this phrase. He frequently uses it in his writing and conversation.

[20]James A. Smith, Sr., and Tammi Ledbetter, "Preaching the Word," *Heartland: A Publication of Midwestern Baptist Theological Seminary* (Summer 1997): 3.

[21]Ibid.

[22]See William H. Willimon, "Preaching: Entertainment or Exposition?" *The Christian Century* (February 28, 1992): 204–6.

[23]Scott Black Johnston, "Who Listens to Stories," 10.

[24]David Bartlett, "Story and History: Narratives and Claims," *Interpretation* 45:3 (July 1991): 229–40.

[25]Willimon, "Preaching," 206.

[26]See Richard Lischer on this point. He offers a helpful corrective on narrative preaching in "The Limits of Story," *Interpretation: A Journal of Bible and Theology* 38:1 (January 1984): 31.

[27]Ibid., 29.